CREATED
To Connect

A Christian's Guide to *The Connected Child*

Created by

Dr. Karyn Purvis
with **Michael** *&* **Amy Monroe**

CREATED
To Connect

Created To Connect
Published by Empowered To Connect™
www.empoweredtoconnect.org
email: info@empoweredtoconnect.org

Third edition. Copyright ©2013 by Karyn Brand Purvis, Michael M. Monroe and Amy S. Monroe

First edition published in 2010. Second edition published in 2011.

All rights reserved. No part of this work may be reproduced in any form for commercial use without written permission from the authors.

Scripture quotations marked NIV are taken from the Holy Bible, New International Version®. Copyright © 1973, 1978, 1984 by International Bible Society. Used by permission of Zondervan. All rights reserved.

Scripture quotations marked The Message are taken from The Message. Copyright © 1993, 1994, 1995, 1996, 2000, 2001, 2002. Used by permission of NavPress Publishing Group.

Editing and interior design: Scott & Annie McClellan
Cover design: Matt Donovan

ISBN: 978-0-615-38225-8

Contents

Preface		1
Introduction		2
1	Hope and Healing	6
2	Where Your Child Began	12
3	Solving the Puzzle of Difficult Behavior	20
4	Disarming the Fear Response with Felt Safety	26
5	Teaching Life Values	32
6	You Are the Boss	36
7	Dealing with Defiance	44
8	Nurturing at Every Opportunity	50
9	Proactive Strategies to Make Life Easier	56
10	Supporting Healthy Brain Chemistry	62
11	Handling Setbacks	66
12	Healing Yourself to Heal Your Child	72

PREFACE

This study guide is written as a companion to *The Connected Child*, a book that I co-authored in 2007 with my colleagues, Dr. David Cross and Wendy Lyons Sunshine. In preparing this study guide I have joined with new journey mates—Michael and Amy Monroe who lead Tapestry (www.tapestryministry.org), the adoption and foster care ministry at Irving Bible Church in Irving, Texas. For years Michael and Amy, themselves adoptive parents of four children, have walked alongside hundreds of families in order to help them find the information, support and, most important of all, the personal connections they need to successfully navigate the adoption and foster care journey. Together, our vision is to see churches everywhere better informed and more fully equipped to empower parents to connect with their children and grow spiritually.

This study guide is an important part of a larger and broader initiative that we are calling Empowered To Connect. Through its user-friendly website (www.empoweredtoconnect.org), Empowered To Connect offers an online library of resources that are highly relevant for adoptive and foster parents, as well as anyone who desires to understand more about the principles and strategies detailed in *The Connected Child*. In addition, Empowered To Connect has created a parent training and regularly conducts conferences and workshops to better prepare and equip families and churches for the adoption and foster care journey. Our heart is that these resources will be useful tools and tremendous sources of encouragement for churches and families alike.

I also want to offer a brief explanation about the way we have written this study guide. While the voice that we have used in this study guide is primarily mine (the I's in this guide refer to me), it has certainly been a joint labor of love among all of us—Michael, Amy and me. We are also grateful for the important contributions of many others who have helped to make this resource a reality—including Scott and Annie McClellan, Matt Donovan and Jason Weber, just to name a few. It has truly been a team effort.

Finally, we want to thank you for allowing us to share in your journey. We pray blessings on you and your family, and we hope that you will be encouraged and empowered by what you discover in these pages.

Karyn B. Purvis, PhD.

INTRODUCTION

*Then you will call, and the Lord will answer;
You will cry for help, and he will say: Here am I.*

— Isaiah 58:9 (NIV)

The longing of the human heart is to connect and belong. We long to connect with our Creator, in whose image we have been made, and by God's grace such a connection is possible. As relational beings we also have a deep need and desire to connect with those around us. One of the most important and meaningful human connections is undoubtedly between a parent and a child.

Our purpose for writing this study guide is to illuminate the biblical foundation and background that support the guiding principles set out in *The Connected Child*. In that sense, I am often asked if *The Connected Child* is a "Christian book." If that question is meant to try and fit the book into the category of books published by a Christian publisher and written exclusively for a Christian audience, including in its pages frequent references to Scripture, my answer is that the book does not fit that standard definition of a "Christian book." If, however, that question is meant to determine whether or not the principles of *The Connected Child* are consistent with Scripture and if the very motivation for my work begins with and grows out of my own personal faith and my steadfast belief that the grace of God can redeem not only our broken spiritual condition but also our physical and relational brokenness, well, my answer is an emphatic, "YES!"

This study guide is designed as a companion to *The Connected Child*, a book co-authored with my colleagues Dr. David Cross and Wendy Lyons Sunshine. This study guide complements the book and I believe you will gain most from this resource if you also spend meaningful time reading and reflecting on what we have written in *The Connected Child*. Each chapter of this study guide contains insights, Scripture, new stories, illustrations, and information that will help you better understand and apply what we introduced and explained in *The Connected Child*. We believe that as you work through these pages—whether by yourself, with a spouse or as part of a small group—you will better understand the philosophy and approach for the holistic model of parenting that we advocate, which has brought hope and healing to countless children and parents. As you do, our prayer is that you will develop a closer connection not only with your children, but also with your Heavenly Father.

Children from Hard Places

The Connected Child and this study guide were written to help you better understand the challenges and needs of "children from hard places." Additionally, these resources, together with the many other resources on the Empowered To Connect website (www.empoweredtoconnect.org), are aimed at providing the necessary insights and tools to help children heal and become whole. Maybe you have already adopted or are currently a foster parent; maybe you are considering adoption or foster care or are in the waiting stage; maybe you are a social worker, orphan care provider or caregiver; or maybe you simply want to understand better how to connect with at-risk children. Regardless of your motivation, we believe these resources can help prepare and equip you to better love, serve and care for the children that God has brought into your life.

Our research and that of others has revealed that there are six primary risk factors that are predictors of children from hard places. These risk factors are: prenatal stress, difficult or traumatic labor or birth, medical trauma early in life, abuse, neglect, and trauma. Based on this list, it is clear that this term, "children from hard places," accurately describes many more children than merely those who were institutionalized or adopted later in life. Further, it is well established that children impacted by adoption or foster care have all experienced relational loss and, as a result, are more likely to encounter a variety of questions and wrestle with different issues relating to that loss and the grief and pain that flow from it. With so much seemingly working against these children and those who love them, it may be tempting to feel defeated and believe there is little hope.

Do not despair—there is hope! As we wrote in the opening chapter of *The Connected Child*, "if you're ready to help your adopted child not just behave but blossom and to empower the healing connections that will bring greater joy to your family," this study guide (and this journey) is for you. There is an undeniable truth that everyone who loves a child from the hard places must remember: *the past affects the future ... but it does not determine it.* It is this foundational truth, and a steadfast faith in and dependence on the One who delights in redeeming and restoring the brokenness of this world, that we pray will sustain and offer you lasting hope as you travel to the mountaintops and through the valleys of this journey.

At the same time, it is important to remember that we do not offer a magic formula or a quick fix. Instead we offer hope born of experience and proven tools that are supported by research. This research and experience makes clear that children can make tremendous strides in overcoming these challenges, and you are an unmistakable part of God's plan to help this happen. With that in mind, our goal is nothing less than to empower you to become a healer for your child, and in so doing, rediscover the joy in parenting. Through this process, you will have the privilege of empowering your child to fulfill all that God has called him to be and to do.

Returning to Old Wisdom

In many ways, my book and this study guide represent a kind of homecoming for me and my work. *The Connected Child* was born out of years of seeking to understand and apply God's practical mercies in the lives of adopted, foster and at-risk children. Our desire is that in this guide you will discover a deeper sense of the mercy and grace that is found only in the presence of our loving God, and that in His presence you will find hope and strength for the journey.

The wisdom of Solomon's words certainly applies to this book and our work—"there is nothing new under the sun" (Ecclesiastes 1:9, NIV). We take no credit for creating the interventions we teach. Rather, in many ways we have simply harnessed the practical wisdom of parents from generations past and combined it with a wealth of research findings from the last 50 years. In that sense, I believe we have proven the old adage to be true—good research scientifically documents the truths that your grandmother knew instinctively.

The Connected Child is essentially a synthesis of this wisdom rooted in Scripture, practiced by generations of parents and applied in helping children make healthy and healing connections. My work for the past decade, together with my colleague Dr. David Cross, has been in developing interventions for at-risk children, and in that process we have synthesized a holistic approach to parenting wounded and hurting children that we refer to as the Trust Based Relational Intervention™ (TBRI) model (developed through the Institute of Child Development (www.child.tcu.edu) at Texas Christian University). I believe that this parenting style reflects God's love for us as His children. His love for us is made tangible in practical ways, and we believe that our parenting must also make our love for our children tangible in practical ways that they can understand, accept and apply.

The Balancing Act

As you engage with the insights and information in these pages we ask that you do so with an open mind and a receptive heart. A temptation for some Christian parents is to use lectures, sermons and even Scripture itself as their only means of admonishing, teaching and correcting, thinking this is God's prescribed way for them to relate to their children. Always quick to correct, they administer harsh and swift punishments based on rules and laws, but neither they nor their children find joy in their shared relationship. Others are prone to err on the side of "cheap grace." Compelled by their children's early histories, these parents don't want to ask too much; tragically, their permissive relationship fails to create trust in their children.

In this study guide we want to point you to a different way—a way that we believe is far better and a way that we are confident will help you better reflect the heart of God for us and your heart of love for your child. Our children need a balance of equal parts nurture and structure and we would do well to look at how Jesus taught and interacted with people as our guide and model for connecting with our children. Always mindful of the whole needs of the people with whom he interacted, when Jesus taught a hungry crowd he was also moved with compassion to feed them and heal their sick. As Jesus taught his disciples, Scripture is replete with examples of how he relied upon stories about nature and parables about human behavior to relate to both their hearts and minds. And when he stood with Mary and Martha at their brother's tomb, he wept with them, even as he surely knew he was about to raise their brother from the dead. Jesus often quoted Scripture, but just as often he used stories about life and the surrounding creation to teach his followers in tangible ways they could understand and apply. Even in his last days on this earth, Jesus was focused on connecting with those around him.

It is our greatest hope and desire that this study guide will empower you with practical tools and insights that allow you to mirror the love of God as you build stronger and more meaningful connections with your children.

CHAPTER 1
Hope and Healing

"For I know the plans I have for you," declares the Lord, "plans to prosper you and not to harm you, plans to give you hope and a future."

— Jeremiah 29:11 (NIV)

Hope. It's a little word with lots of meaning and many different meanings at that. Hope is something everyone wants and certainly needs. Without hope there is little reason to go on, as in the saying that signals the bitter end—"when all hope is lost." With hope and for hope people persevere and do extraordinary things, even though it may seem to some that the situation is "beyond all hope." And when hope proves to be merely "false hope" or hope seemingly fails, it can be discouraging and at times even devastating. The question is not whether hope is important in our lives, but rather what exactly is hope and how can we find it.

Over the years we've heard many parents say things such as, "We were so sure God called us to adopt our son, but we don't understand why nothing we do seems to work! He just keeps getting worse and worse. We're at the end of our rope!" We are talking about good, faithful people who are devoted and committed and want nothing more than to be good parents and to raise healthy, happy children who love God and love others. These parents started the adoption or foster care journey confident, joyful and full of hope, but all too soon came to the point of questioning their decisions, their ability and whether they ever really heard God's voice at all. Feeling alone, frustrated and defeated, they begin to lose hope as they struggle to survive and simply endure the challenges of each new day.

Hope for the Whole Child

In our respective roles as researcher/teacher and church ministry leaders we've had the privilege to walk with many families as they discovered and re-discovered the joy of parenting. Central to this is helping parents become aware of and focus on the "whole child."

In the days of the Old Testament, devout Hebrew fathers would stand facing Jerusalem several times each day and recite the Shema: "Hear, O Israel: The Lord our God, the Lord is one. Love the Lord your God with all your heart and with all your soul and with all your strength" (Deuteronomy 6:5, NIV). In response to a religious expert's question about what was the greatest commandment, Jesus replied by also quoting the Shema, and adding to it a second command—to love your neighbor as yourself (Matthew 22:39).

In this way, Scripture teaches us something very important about how we have been created to relate and be related to. Jesus made it clear that we are to love God and others with our whole selves—the same way we need to be loved. Similarly, we encourage parents to cultivate an awareness of the "whole being" of their child. This requires that they be mindful of their child's "heart, mind, soul and strength" even as they learn to fully embrace their child's past, present and future. By loving and nurturing our children in this holistic way we can give them the gift of "real hope"—an opportunity to heal and become whole—even as we teach them about and point them toward the source of everlasting hope in Jesus Christ.

Keeping a Grip on Hope

The period following the destruction of Jerusalem in 586 B.C. was a "dark" time for the Jews in Babylonian exile. It was a time of great suffering and seemingly little hope, yet in the midst of these circumstances Jeremiah wrote these words:

I'll never forget the trouble, the utter lostness,
  the taste of ashes, the poison I've swallowed.
I remember it all—oh, how well I remember—
  the feeling of hitting the bottom.
But there's one other thing I remember,
  and remembering, I keep a grip on hope:
God's loyal love couldn't have run out,
  his merciful love couldn't have dried up.
They're created new every morning.
  How great your faithfulness!
I'm sticking with God (I say it over and over).
  He's all I've got left.
It's a good thing to quietly hope,
  quietly hope for help from God.

— Lamentations 3:19-24, 26 (*The Message*)

Questions to Consider and Discuss:

1. Looking at this passage of Scripture, where is the author of these words placing his hope? What does he "remember" when he begins to "lose hope"?

2. Thinking about your adoption or foster care journey, what challenges or issues have you encountered (or do you expect to encounter) that have caused (or could cause) you to lose hope?

3. What are some things that we as parents need to "remember" (i.e., focus on and keep in mind) in order to keep our "grip on hope"?

4. What aspects of your "whole child" do you sometimes overlook or fail to embrace? How might being more holistic actually become a source of hope and healing for you and your child?

The Gardens of Life
By Cheryl Macdonald

We moved into our current home about two years ago, and as with any previously owned home there were a few not so welcome surprises. These unwelcomed surprises were easily overcome, however, by the beautiful landscaping, in particular the well-planned and maintained backyard garden, that we inherited with our new home.

Surrounding our stone pool deck is a lovely haven of green boasting an array of interesting flowers and trees. From the four varieties of roses to the multitude of crape myrtles, lilies and blooming hedges, color graces our little backyard retreat virtually year round. While maintaining our backyard garden requires some effort, we humbly admit that most of it existed long before we claimed it as "ours."

As the seasons change we love the new surprises that seemingly bloom to greet us—lovely things we did not plant and therefore are delighted to discover. There are, however, other things in our garden we most certainly did not plant. Take for instance the parasitic vine that continually fights for a corner with my Indian Hawthorne or the patch of dandelions in the yard that seem to be resistant to any effort to eradicate them. For a while I was convinced they actually multiplied when weed killer was applied. In order to preserve and protect the intended beauty of the garden we've had to call the "weed man" for professional advice about the right intervention.

The Garden of My Daughter's Heart and Life
Our precious daughter came home in December 2006. We celebrated her 12th birthday just a few weeks later, and she has been a joy and a blessing to our family in so many ways. As her "roots"

deepen in the "soil" of our family, I have come to appreciate and respect the garden of her heart and life. This garden was planted and blossoming long before I knew her name or became her mother. There are so many beautiful things in the garden of my daughter's heart and life—lovely things I did not plant! I was not there to see her first step, her first time to run, jump or climb, yet I have discovered that she is an amazingly fast, skilled athlete, and a graceful dancer. I did not hear her first words, but she has incredible language skills and is fluent in both English and Russian. Once she was home I discovered she could crochet, sew and cook. I have come to admire her strong work ethic, exhibited through diligence and determination—all qualities modeled for her half a world away. And I did not teach her to read, ride a bicycle or build snowmen, yet she loves to keep illustrated journals, ride bikes with no hands and build astounding things out of snow.

As with my backyard garden, there are also other things in the garden of my daughter's heart and life that I did not plant but cannot ignore. There are hard things that do not give life and instead seem intent to steal the beauty and joy from her victories. There are the fast-growing vines of fear and loss that try to choke out the trust and sense of permanence that has blossomed between us. And then there is the stubborn root of self-reliance that impedes vulnerability and healthy attachment. Nurturing the beauty and healthy growth in my daughter's heart and life requires constant vigilance, regular work and the humility and willingness to call upon and utilize available resources (much like the "weed man") when needed.

In this ongoing effort to help bring forth our daughter's beauty and hold at bay the "weeds" in her life, I've relied upon amazing support from other adoptive families and our church, as well as books, conferences and skilled counselors. But by far the most valuable resource—for me and for her—is the Master Gardener. The garden in our backyard did not come to be by chance. It was carefully designed and created for a purpose. The same is true of our daughter. Acknowledging God as the One who designed her unique and precious life has created a bridge from her past to the present and enables us to continue traveling this journey toward a hope-filled future. He knows better than anyone, including my daughter herself, what things are buried deep in the garden of her heart, and He desires to see those things that He planted burst into life and beautiful color.

As the seasons of life change I know there will be many more surprises that will blossom forth from my daughter's heart and life. Some will spring forth with life and beauty; others will seek an unsuspecting moment to yield patches of doubt and insecurity. Trusting His skill and purpose gives me courage and hope as I watch my daughter's heart and life bloom and stand amazed at His master plan.

Real Hope in the Balance

The challenges, problems and pain that our children face are real, and as a result, they affect us as parents too. These challenges impact the whole child; therefore, we must be willing to engage and embrace our children (and ourselves!) holistically. At the same time, we must always remember there are no quick fixes—merely changing behaviors will not accomplish what is needed most. Our goal must be nothing less than healing for the whole child. Much like our own journey of spiritual healing and maturity, the healing we desire for our children will be a process, and it must be anchored by hope—*real hope*.

Fundamental to this real hope is an understanding that our children need a healthy and consistent balance of both nurture (affection, compassion, mercy) and structure (rules, limits, boundaries). Put another way, our children need a balance between connecting (nurture) and correcting (structure). As a result, the challenge is to identify what your child is really saying and what your child really needs. If we give a child structure (rules and correction) when she needs nurture (affection and mercy), we damage her ability to trust. If we give a child nurture when she needs structure, we limit her ability to grow. Therefore, we must learn to see our children and understand what they need in all of their being.

I believe this is similar to how God relates to us as His children. Using a balance of both nurture (His tender mercies) and structure (His guiding hand directing and correcting), He kindly, yet firmly, leads us into a right relationship with Him. I love the way *The Message* reflects the words of Paul in describing how God handles us, His children: "God is kind, but he's not soft. In kindness he takes us firmly by the hand and leads us into a radical life-change" (Romans 2:4). As parents, we too must lovingly, intentionally and firmly take our children by the hand and lead them into a relationship of trust and healing. It is through this process, and as a result of this renewed relationship, that we and our children will discover real, life-changing hope.

More Questions to Consider and Discuss:

1. Thinking back to Cheryl's story, "The Gardens of Life," what are some of the beautiful things (i.e., characteristics, traits, qualities, etc.) that are present in your child's life? What are some of the "weeds" in your child's life that need to be attended to?

2. What are some of the ways God has nurtured (i.e., connected with) you in your relationship with Him? What are some ways He has provided structure for (i.e., corrected) you?

3. Who are the people in your life that have cared for and related to you with this balance of nurture and structure? How did they do it? What impact did it have?

4. Think of an example when your child might have needed or even been asking for (whether with words or behaviors) one type of interaction (nurture or structure) and you provided the other. What was the result for him/her? What was the result for you?

Chapter 2
Where Your Child Began

I praise you because I am fearfully and wonderfully made; your works are wonderful, I know that full well.

— Psalm 139:14 (NIV)

For many families, the arrival of a child is met with eager anticipation. Welling with joy and excitement, these parents' lives and actions toward their child manifest a deep awareness that children truly are a gift from God (Psalm 127:3)! Cradled gently, touched adoringly and nurtured sacrificially, the child learns to see himself through the mirror of his parents' eyes. "I am precious," "I am safe," and "I am loved" become the song of his heart. Ultimately, his inheritance of faith will be in knowing that he is "fearfully and wonderfully made" (Psalms 139:14) and deeply loved by a compassionate and merciful Heavenly Father. As a strong and secure attachment is created with loving parents, this child will be well prepared to develop trust and create healthy relationships as he begins to explore the world, as well as to "attach" in faith to the loving God who created him in His image. His earliest moments of life become the foundation for what he will come to know and believe about himself, his parents, his world and his God!

Starting at the Beginning for Your Child

Researchers have documented the profound and lasting effects that early care or the lack thereof have on the development of trust ("I am safe"), self-worth ("I am precious") and self-efficacy ("I am heard"). In addition, developmental researchers widely acknowledge that the formative early days dramatically influence attachment relationships and also have dramatic and lasting effects on brain development and brain chemistry. Tragically, many of the children that we love and serve came into an unwelcoming world and started life amidst very difficult circumstances. Disease, abandonment, hunger, mental illness, stress, substance abuse and a host of other risk factors may have conspired to create an environment where these children's needs were unmet, contributing to the abuse, neglect and trauma that they experienced. These heartbreaking early harms and losses often hold our children back from developing in healthy or optimal ways and too often prevent them from developing trust and understanding just how precious they truly are.

For some of our children, their "histories" are known, at least in part. For many others, however, their "histories" are unknown, even though we know their past almost certainly involves some degree of harm, deprivation or loss. Whether it is abuse, neglect or some other known harm, or whether it is the likelihood of a difficult or stressful pregnancy, difficult labor or birth, early medical trauma or a ruptured attachment to an early caregiver, the impacts for our children can be significant. You've heard it said, "What you don't know can't hurt you." Unfortunately, it is often what we don't know (and may never know) that is in fact hurting our children, and therefore hurting us as well. As a result, adoptive and foster parents must be particularly insightful about the reality of their child's history and the lingering effects it can have.

So what do we do in light of this? First and foremost we must be willing to approach our children with genuine compassion, both for their histories as well as the challenges they are still facing. As we lead our children along the journey toward healing, this compassion must always be our touchstone. That is not to say that our children do not need appropriate levels and expressions of structure and correction—they most certainly do. But we must never forget that our children need this structure and correction expressed compassionately, in ways they can understand and in ways that promote lasting healing and connection.

*Seeing Our Children with Eyes of Compassion**

Question: We returned home with our child (adopted internationally) about three weeks ago. We are finding the adjustment much more difficult than we expected. For example, she is nearly 10 months old and is still not sleeping through the night. In addition, she cries all the time and is very irritable and unhappy in general. Frankly, it is making it very difficult for us to feel connected to her, and we are growing frustrated and tired. What are we doing wrong, and what should we consider in order to get things back to normal?

The Empowered To Connect Team Responds: The question about your daughter is a familiar one. I understand your frustration and can only imagine how tired—physically and emotionally—you must be, not only from the past three weeks, but also from your recent international travel and even from the adoption process that likely lasted many months or even years.

In dealing with this, however, it is helpful for parents to think in terms of the loss and grief process that occurs for children when they leave all that is familiar and all that they know to come home to families in the U.S. That is most certainly what your daughter has experienced. Thinking in terms of her experience, there have been drastic changes in virtually everything that was comforting and familiar to her: language, voices, faces, foods, smells and sounds. In addition we know from research that it can be difficult on a child to move at any age, especially between eight and 12 months of age. This is the period of time when their first attachment is forming, and it is one of the most critical periods of time in all of child development. As a result, she will need lots of nurturing, loving care in order to bridge the shocking change that happened "overnight" for her (although you and your wife have been planning it for a long time).

In order to help children like your daughter successfully transition during this critical time, I encourage parents to stay at home with a new child as much as possible for a minimum of 30 to 40 days, and I prefer three months whenever possible. During this time, your daughter's needs should be the primary focus. In meeting those needs consistently and lovingly, you are helping her settle in for a lifetime and giving her a foundation and a practical understanding of what it means to be part of a loving, forever family!

So my encouragement to you is to hold her when she cries and take time with her in the night because these next three months offer the best opportunity for teaching her trust and helping her develop the foundation for a secure and healthy attachment. Developmentally, this is when she will learn trust ("My parents will meet my needs!"), self-worth ("My needs are met, so I must be precious!") and self-efficacy ("My cries matter because someone comes when I cry!"). In that respect, these months are without a doubt the most important days you will ever spend with her. With that in mind, I hope that you are encouraged that the "return" on your investment is not all that far away, and you and your daughter will certainly be the better for you having made it.

Adapted from a post on Empowered To Connect at www.empoweredtoconnect.org/resources.

Key Scripture Verses

In reply Jesus said: "A man was going down from Jerusalem to Jericho when he fell into the hands of robbers. They stripped him of his clothes, beat him and went away, leaving him half dead. A priest happened to be going down the same road, and when he saw the man, he passed by on the other side. So too, a Levite, when he came to the place and saw him, passed by on the other side. But a Samaritan, as he traveled, came where the man was; and when he saw him, he took pity on him. He went to him and bandaged his wounds, pouring on oil and wine. Then he put the man on his own donkey, took him to an inn and took care of him. The next day he took out two silver coins and gave them to the innkeeper. 'Look after him,' he said, 'and when I return, I will reimburse you for any extra expense you may have.'" "Which of these three do you think was a neighbor to the man who fell into the hands of robbers?" The expert in the law replied, "The one who had mercy on him." Jesus told him, "Go and do likewise."

—Luke 10:30-37 (NIV)

More Than a Feeling

We see in Scripture that compassion and mercy for the wounded, oppressed and less fortunate are hallmarks of what God expects from His people. This is evident throughout Jesus' ministry as he healed the sick and reached out to the outcast, and advocated that his followers do the same. This is probably best reflected in his answer to the question, "Who is my neighbor?" recorded in Luke 10. In response, Jesus tells the Parable of the Good Samaritan, and it is in this story that we clearly see some of the key elements that define this kind of tangible and restorative compassion.

In this story Jesus tells of a man that was robbed on the road from Jericho to Jerusalem. Beaten and left for dead, both a priest and a Levite (a religious man) encountered him but both passed him by. Finally, a Samaritan passed by and in this Samaritan's response to the beaten man's condition we see a model of true compassion.

First, we learn that compassion is rooted in genuine concern and understanding of another person's hurt and need. In the story, upon seeing the injured man, the Samaritan "took pity on him" (verse

33). *The Message* says that the Samaritan's "heart went out to him."

Second, we discover that true compassion moves us to action. The Samaritan's compassion did not stop at a mere feeling, no matter how genuine that feeling may have been. After all, for all we know the priest and the Levite before him might have felt pity for the injured man as well, but they were unwilling to allow their feelings to move them toward action—actions that reflect the kind of compassion that can bring healing, restoration and wholeness. Moved to action, however, the Samaritan stopped and went to the wounded man, bandaged his wounds and then carried him to an inn (verse 34). In this way, the Samaritan put his compassion into action.

Finally, we see that compassion calls for us to engage in an ongoing process that is focused on bringing about healing and restoration. It is important to see that the Samaritan was not content to merely have genuine feelings toward the beaten man, nor to merely "stop the bleeding" and get him to safety. Instead, Jesus goes out of his way to tell us that after they arrived at the inn the Samaritan "took care of him," and the next morning he made arrangements for his ongoing care until his promised return (verse 35). It is in light of the Samaritan's tangible and ongoing response of compassion that Jesus instructs those who were listening (and us) to "go and do likewise" (verse 37).

Questions to Consider and Discuss:

1. Why do you think the priest and the Levite did not stop?

2. What causes us as parents not to "stop" and remember that our children who come from "hard places" are very likely scared, hurting and in need of this kind of restorative compassion?

3. Of the three aspects of compassion highlighted in the Parable of the Good Samaritan (i.e., having genuine concern, stopping and acting, and engaging in an ongoing process of healing and restoration), what is the most difficult one for you to consistently exhibit in response to your child? Why?

4. The Samaritan's opportunity to show love and compassion for the injured man arose because of the harm and pain the man had suffered at the hands of the robbers. In some ways the same is true for adoptive and foster parents: our children's painful histories have played a significant role in bringing our lives together. In light of this, consider the role compassion should play as you parent your child. How does this perspective change your view of your child's past? How does this perspective change your view of your role as your child's parent?

Returning to the Beginning

As we begin to understand the loss and pain of our precious ones who have come from "hard places," we have the opportunity to put our compassion into action and be used by God to help bring them much needed hope and healing. It is precisely this kind of tangible compassion that will help our children more fully realize their God-given worth and preciousness that was previously obscured by the legacy of pain, confusion and frustration from their difficult past.

For younger children, this calls for a great deal of extra and intentional affection (such as holding, rocking and feeding), kindness and patience from parents. At the same time, these children will need a healthy balance of appropriate rules, structure and boundaries, but always provided in a way that gives voice, builds trust and promotes connection. It is this balance of nurture and structure (which we will focus on in more detail in Chapter 6) that can best provide them what they need to develop trust, establish strong connections and heal.

For older children, parents need to understand that they may actually be required to "go backwards" in order to move forward. One mother who adopted an 11 year-old girl from Eastern Europe recalled how her daughter, having just arrived in the U.S. after living in an orphanage nearly all of her life, wanted to have hot tea together five to six times every day. At first the mom was dismayed and more than a little frustrated, but then she recalled how many hundreds of bottles and sippy cups she had prepared for her biological children over the years. For her new daughter, the repetitive hot tea ritual was not really about tea at all. It was about being nurtured, experiencing love and establishing a deeper connection. It was her daughter's way of making up for some of what had been missed. In that context, six cups of hot tea every day for weeks, even months, was certainly worth the return on the investment.

As we look at our children holistically with eyes of compassion and as we live out that compassion in tangible and practical ways that our children can understand, we have the opportunity to bless our children in unimaginable ways. For many of our children, their past has profoundly and negatively affected every aspect of their being. To help them move forward, we need to have "all of them" in mind as we patiently and compassionately love them.

Be Compassionate!*

We ask parents who have adopted children from "hard places" to be aware of the implications of non-optimal care on developing children. Before we can provide these children with a message of safety and love, we must first learn to "speak their language." In order to do that, it is imperative that we have insight about neural and sensory development and possible alterations in belief systems, which may significantly affect behavior and attachment.

Neural sub-systems issues: An example of understanding neural development through the lens of compassion can be found in viewing children's idiosyncratic behaviors and beliefs. Children adopted before the age of two rarely have retrievable memories of their experiences. However, if they experienced hunger, loneliness or fear during this time, they may exhibit a chronic and pervasive sense of hunger, loneliness or fear. Their brain development was not complete enough for them to form tangible memories the way four or five-year-old children might. Yet in spite of now living in safe homes

16 Created to Connect

with adoring parents, these children may be haunted by overwhelming feelings of being unloved. Paradoxical as it may seem, children with concrete memories of their hardships are often easier to guide. They can learn to "use their words" to talk about pre-adoptive memories (e.g., "I was hungry, and there wasn't enough food," or "I was lonely, and I wanted to be held and no one was there for me").

Those children with tangible memories can learn to use their words to tell their stories and to be released from the power of early experiences. But for younger children who experience harm before brain maturation can facilitate tangible memories, the journey for healing can be frustrating for both parents and children. However, in time and with consistent, compassionate care, parents who understand their children's neurological issues can guide little ones to the truth that they are safe, loved and deeply cared for!

We invite parents to ask two questions when they observe behaviors that seem unacceptable or idiosyncratic. The first question is, "What is your child really saying?" And the second is, "What does your child really need?"

Sensory sub-systems issues: Sensory processing deficits are another common outcome for children who fail to experience optimal care during the early months of life. Sensory processing deficits can cause children to misunderstand their environment in ways that result in them misinterpreting social cues, facial expressions and the meaning of touches and hugs (to name a few). In these things, parents must be informed about how sensory issues can be addressed and treated, and must also understand behavioral manifestations of sensory processing issues. We recommend the book *The Out of Sync Child* by Carol Kranowitz, which clearly describes each of the "internal senses," how sensory defensiveness manifests and how we can effectively intervene at home and school.

We encourage parents to be compassionate toward the behavioral issues that might be associated with sensory-processing deficits. For example, a newly adopted child who is tactile-defensive may not want to be hugged or touched. Although this is a painful experience for parents (and is often mistaken for attachment problems), this deficit can be effectively treated. However, it will require compassionate patience on the part of the parent. A similar corollary to a child who does not want to be hugged due to tactile defensiveness is the child who has a proprioceptive deficit and yelps when his parents hug him, claiming that they are hurting him. This hypersensitivity to physical pressure can also be effectively addressed (for specific information, see *The Out of Sync Child*).

Belief sub-system issues: Adopted children very frequently develop belief systems associated with their experiences with early caregivers. Those belief systems may include beliefs like "I am not loveable," "Adults can't be trusted," or "If I had value, I wouldn't have been given away." It is important for adoptive parents to be compassionate toward the children's belief systems while gently leading them to know the truth—that they are beautiful, precious, valuable and loved!

We ask parents in their compassionate responses toward their child to honor the child's history while giving the child a hope for the future. For example, if the child did not receive adequate nutrition during early development, they may "hear" a message of hunger that causes them to hoard or steal food. In this circumstance, a parent can say, "It is true that you were hungry many times before you came home, but my promise is that you will never be hungry in our home. But, you may not steal or hide food. Anytime that you are hungry, come to me and I will go to the kitchen with you and you may sit and eat whatever you are hungry for. If you would like, I will even take you to the grocery story and let you choose your favorite snacks and nuts and fruit to put in a basket in your room." In these ways we show compassion toward our children while bringing them out of their pre-adoptive history and into the complete safety of our home and our love. By being attentive to neurological and sensory issues and residual belief systems, compassionate parents can more easily navigate their children's histories and understand their children's language.

*Adapted from "Six Words for Adoptive Parents to Live By" by Dr. Karyn Purvis and Dr. David Cross.

More Questions to Consider and Discuss:

1. Thinking in terms of the Parable of the Good Samaritan and taking into account your child's history (both what you know and what you don't), in what ways is your child "injured and bleeding" on the side of the road — emotionally, physically, relationally? In light of this, what does Jesus' command to "go and do likewise" mean for you as the parent of this child?

2. What are some of the things that can keep you from having this kind of compassion toward your child?

3. What do you need to keep in mind as you seek to be truly compassionate toward your child?

4. How can you best show compassion toward your child even when you don't feel compassionate?

Chapter 3
Solving the Puzzle of Difficult Behavior

Jesus said, "Let the little children come to me, and do not hinder them, for the kingdom of heaven belongs to such as these."

— Matthew 19:14 (NIV)

As the disciples looked out over the gathering crowd of children, with their soil-smudged little faces and hands, they must have been dismayed. After all, Jesus was on a mission to establish his father's kingdom, so there was little time to spend (or waste) with the children whose mothers had brought them in hopes of seeing and being blessed by Jesus.

In Scripture, scenes like this often conjure in our minds a picture of children sitting patiently, each quiet and neatly dressed, as they wait their turn for a few moments with Jesus. No doubt you have seen the Sunday school paintings depicting the meek and mild Jesus sitting with calm children gathered around listening attentively. But if the children that were brought to Jesus were like most, and certainly they were, it is just as likely they were running, jumping and playing. In other words, they were being regular kids. In fact, I suspect that many of them were being less than saintly, only serving to further the disciples' frustration.

There is a reason (maybe several reasons) that Matthew seems to go out of his way to record this brief scene in his gospel account. He tells us that the disciples rebuked those who brought the children to Jesus, presumably intent on "protecting" Jesus from this unruly crowd of little ones who the disciples saw as merely a distraction from the important business Jesus had to do. So imagine their confusion when Jesus insisted that the children come to him, and having blessed them declared that the kingdom belonged to "such as these." The disciples could not see past the children's behavior, their lowly status and their simple humanity. Jesus, however, could not help but look beyond these things to see their preciousness, their potential and their childlike faith.

Seeing Beyond the Obvious

Examples such as this were commonplace during the earthly ministry of Jesus. He was never content to dwell merely on the surface of things, focusing on the obvious and outward. He understood that what lay beneath the surface was what really mattered. The change Jesus sought, and the change that he knew people needed, started at the center (their heart) and transformed them, sometimes albeit slowly, from the inside out.

The same challenge and opportunity exists for parents. It is often difficult, sometimes seemingly impossible, to see beyond our children's behaviors. And yet, that is exactly what children—particularly those from hard places—need for us to do. Our children desperately need parents who can see beyond their behaviors to the real child that is locked inside a fortress of fear, confusion and shame.

At the same time, it is important to keep in mind that "seeing beyond" our children's behaviors is not the same as overlooking behaviors that are unhealthy, unacceptable and hold them back. Some parents at this point may be tempted to respond, "How can we just let our children get away with bad behavior? Isn't it our responsibility to teach them right and wrong and to discipline them accordingly?" The answer is certainly yes, but as we seek to do this it is important that we remain focused on the primary goal.

Every parent needs to answer the fundamental question: "What is my primary goal?" Is it merely to achieve good or right behavior? If so, this focus will largely shape how we as parents approach our children and the interactions we have with them (specifically, how we approach connecting and correcting). But if our primary goal is to build a strong and healthy relationship—a connection with our children that serves as a strong foundation and enables them to develop trust, heal from past wounds and experience a deep sense of felt safety, self-worth and empowerment—then our approach and interactions will likely look different. I believe this is God's goal for us—that we grow deeper in our relationship with Him (Matthew 22:37) and from that our desires, thoughts and actions begin to reflect the character of His Son. Likewise, we believe that our kids need, and almost every parent desires, this kind of strong foundation of connection. The key, therefore, is to not allow your child's bad behavior to distract you from building this foundation that will allow true healing and growth to occur.

Questions to Consider and Discuss:

1. Why is it sometimes difficult to "see beyond" your child's behaviors?

2. What is your primary goal as a parent? How does your relationship with your child, particularly in terms of how you handle connecting and correcting, reflect or correspond to this goal?

3. What tends to distract you as a parent from achieving this goal?

Getting to the Heart of the Matter

Turning again to Jesus as our guide, we find that he never excused or condoned behavior that "missed the mark." But we also discover that he seldom lectured, scolded or preached at those who were hurting and in need of help and healing. Instead, he looked beyond the surface to the "root cause" in order to offer true hope. We must also be willing to do the same with our children. No example better illustrates this than the Samaritan woman's life-changing encounter with Jesus at Jacob's well.

As recorded in the fourth chapter of John's Gospel, Jesus' encounter with the woman at the well is instructive for us as parents as we deal with our children's behaviors. The woman's failures were clear and apparently well known, but looking beyond the obvious Jesus knew that the woman's sin pointed to a much deeper problem. Given the number and nature of her relationships we can speculate that she was trying to fill some void in her life. Ironically, much like many children from hard places, this woman clearly was seeking a close, connected relationship, but her behaviors were actually preventing her from finding what she sought. Many of our children desperately want to be loved, to feel that they have worth and to feel connected, yet their pain is so deep, the void so large and the confusion so great that they often act in ways that inhibit rather than promote the very thing they desire. Similarly, we also see this with children who act out and seemingly sabotage themselves even as things start to move in a positive direction.

Thankfully, but not surprisingly, we find Jesus interacting with the Samaritan woman in a way that offered her lasting hope and the fulfillment of her deepest needs. While never once condoning or ignoring her behavior, he kept his focus on helping her find what she truly needed—a relationship and a connection that would change her from the inside out. In the same way, our children need to understand God's love for them and the hope that is offered through Jesus Christ, even as they desperately need to experience that love expressed in tangible and practical ways through us.

Seeing the Real Child

By Dr. Karyn Purvis

In spite of our devotion to the Lord, even in our good intentions and clarity of mind, we will at times fail to see the true needs of our child and what is needed most from us as parents. After speaking at an adoption support group in a local church, I was approached by a woman who had responded to God's call to adopt. A faithful believer, sincerely seeking to hear from God and follow as He led, she had come to the group looking for answers but seemingly could find none for herself or her child.

Inna was adopted from an orphanage when she was 11 years old, and her mother was frustrated to tears by her daughter's behaviors. "She is so manipulative; I don't know what to do with her! She calls me every day from school saying she wants me to pick her up. She expects me to drive to school and pick her up and drive her home. She claims she is afraid. Her manipulation is driving me crazy. After all, my (biological) daughter went to the same school and rode her bike back and forth every day without complaining or ever calling me to come pick her up. I just cannot understand why Inna can't do the same."

Sadly, Inna's mother was blinded by her daughter's frustrating and perplexing behaviors. She could not see past them to recall the cruel experiences of Inna's first 11 years of life. As we talked, I asked Inna's mother to recount for me what those early years entailed for Inna. After listening carefully, I gently reminded this loving mother that while her biological daughter had been loved and adored, fed nourishing meals and played with carefree abandon, little Inna, abandoned at birth, had struggled daily for scraps of food. For years the only human attention she received was as the sexual "pet" of the orphanage workers. A beautiful child, Inna was abused day and night by male and female attendants.

No doubt Inna exhibited these troubling behaviors and others that were frustrating to her mother, but they were behaviors born of fear. The fear of riding a bike in the strange neighborhood was a terrifying experience for her and pointed to something much bigger.

"Could I give you another option?" I continued. "Would you consider telling Inna that you will walk her to school every morning and meet her after school every day to walk her home. Tell her she can walk with you or ride her bike beside you. Tell her you will walk her to and from school as long as she needs you to. It may take a week. It may take a month. It may take a year. But sooner or later Inna will ask you to let her try it alone, and in the process, you will have won her heart because you will have built trust and helped her understand that she is safe."

Key Scripture Verses

No doubt many of us have read countless times the great "love passage" in Paul's first letter to the Corinthians. But I wonder how many of us have ever read these words with our child's difficult and challenging behaviors fresh in our mind? Take a few minutes to read and meditate on the verses below (or better yet, read all of 1 Corinthians 13) from your perspective as a parent of a child who, at times, may be very difficult to connect with.

Love is patient, love is kind. It does not envy, it does not boast, it is not proud. It is not rude, it is not self-seeking, it is not easily angered, it keeps no record of wrongs. Love does not delight in evil but rejoices with the truth. It always protects, always trusts, always hopes, always perseveres. Love never fails.

—1 Corinthians 13:4-8 (NIV)

Defining Love In Ways Our Children Can Understand

No one would argue that our children—maybe especially our children—need love. The question (and the challenge) for us as parents is whether we have learned to define that love and are prepared to express it in practical ways they can understand and truly experience. In other words, have we learned to "translate" our love into actions and a way of relating that will bring about connection, healing and transformation, or are we speaking a "foreign" love language that our children are not equipped to interpret, understand and receive?

The real question for us as followers of Christ and those who have been called to the children we now love and serve is "Are we allowing the Spirit of God to do this work in and through us?" Keeping our children's history fully in mind, we need to ask ourselves, "Is our love patient, is it kind, is it self-seeking, is it easily angered, does it keep a record of wrongs, does it always protect, always hope and always persevere? Does our love fail?"

Undoubtedly we will fall short far too often in consistently speaking and living a "love language" that connects with our children in this deeply transforming way. But we all must recognize that what we have been called to is a journey, and we are not meant to travel it alone. God has provided us with helpful resources, insightful people, one another and ultimately His Word and His Spirit as companions and guides for this journey. As we continue to faithfully travel with our children toward healing and wholeness, let us pray that we become increasingly those who, by God's Spirit, are led to love our children as we ourselves are loved by God.

More Questions to Consider and Discuss:

1. What behaviors does your child exhibit that hide the "real child" (i.e., the preciousness and potential of your child that may be "masked" by your child's behaviors)?

2. What characteristics do you believe your child possesses that are "hidden" beneath those behaviors?

3. Think about your recent interactions with your child. In what ways do those interactions look like the kind of love that Paul describes? In what ways do those interactions fall short of that kind of love?

4. What are some specific things that you can do to better live out the kind of love that Paul is describing, even in the face of your child's bad behavior?

Chapter 4
Disarming the Fear Response

There is no room in love for fear. Well-formed love banishes fear. Since fear is crippling, a fearful life—fear of death, fear of judgment—is one not yet fully formed in love. We, though, are going to love—love and be loved. First we were loved, now we love. He loved us first.

— 1 John 4:18-19 (*The Message*)

Fear—it is a crippling and sometimes debilitating feeling, but it is so much more than a feeling. For many children from hard places, fear is a constant, though unwelcome, companion. It is a way of life. From research we know that fear left unaddressed can have pervasive and long-lasting effects on a child, including negative impacts on cognitive ability, sensory processing, brain development, ability to focus and ability to trust. As a result, it distorts and dictates much of what our children are dealing with.

But let's be honest—fear is not something that only our children deal with. Many of us deal with fear and much of that fear relates to our children. We also see time and time again God telling His people through the words of Scripture, "Fear not," and "Do not be afraid." Not only that, we know that love—God's "perfect love"—drives out fear (1 John 4:18). John, of course, was referring to the fear of judgment before God and the confidence that those who have placed their faith and trust in Christ now have. But this all leads us to ask, "What are we to make of the fear that seems to surround our children? What about the fear that seems to surround the adoption and foster care journey in general? How are we to respond to all this fear?"

Finding a New Best Friend for Our Children

To begin to understand fear and its effects, much less begin to deal with it, we need to develop a more complete picture of what it is and what it looks like, particularly for our children. In general, fear is a common and even natural response to people, situations and circumstances that are threatening, unfamiliar or that we don't understand or can't control. And it is important to note that fear can be very real even when what we are afraid of isn't real at all.

Thinking in terms of our children, we must recognize that for many children from hard places, fear is their best friend. Due in large part to their past, fear has ruled their lives—their mind, emotions and behaviors—for so long that it has become a familiar, and even oddly comforting, companion. Rather than having more brain activity in the frontal regions of the brain (i.e., the part of the brain that can process thoughts such as, "I can communicate my needs," "I can communicate my wants," "I can tell you that I am hurt or afraid," etc.), children from hard places often operate in the more primitive part of the brain, called the amygdala. As a result, their behaviors and interactions are more likely to be driven by more primal thoughts such as, "How do I get food?" "How do I get safe?" "How do I get what I want?" and "How do I get my way?" They are stuck in survival mode and, therefore, they are prone to misinterpret communication (both verbal and nonverbal) as threatening and respond in ways that are unacceptable.

To make matters worse, many of our children have become so accustomed to living in a persistent state of fear that they no longer recognize it for what it is. And while it is one of the main obstacles that stands in the way of what we want for our children, it is still a very familiar state of being for them; consequently, many parents encounter surprising and frustrating resistance as they try to help their children confront and move beyond their fear.

In place of this old friend, fear, we need to introduce our children (and ourselves) to a new best friend: trust. In looking at the many times in Scripture that God instructs His people not to be afraid, there is a pattern that often follows. Time and time again, we see God say, "Fear not, I am here," "Fear not, I am with you," and "Do not be afraid, I will help." In these words God is saying, "Do not fear, instead look to me and trust me. I am here and I will help." It is in this repeated invitation to exchange our fear for trust that we find the foundation for what our children (and we ourselves) need in order to escape the grip of fear.

Learning to Trust and Let Go of Fear

So what do you do for a child who has become so accustomed to being fear-filled that he is literally *afraid of not being afraid*? How can you best help this child?

First, we must recognize that the issue is in fact fear itself. As we mentioned before, fear is often chameleon-like in the lives of our children. What many parents immediately interpret as defiance, poor behavior, a rotten attitude, manipulation or immaturity, may actually be driven by a fear response. Often, fear isn't easily identifiable, so it helps to know what you're looking for.

When working with at-risk kids, the vast majority of what we will come to know about them is determined simply from observing them. For example, we know that chronic fear in our children often causes hypervigilance. As a result, we need to be on the lookout for signs of this fear response. When you try to make eye contact, does the child's body become stiff and rigid? Do their hands curl up, do their pupils enlarge, does their jaw tighten? How do they respond to certain sensory inputs such as light, smell or touch? These are just a few of the many ways we can observe if our children are in a constant state of high alert.

Another critical thing that parents can do to help their children combat fear is to understand their child's need for what is called "felt safety." As parents we are often inclined to view a situation or circumstance solely from our own perspective, only taking into account what we know and perceive (all assessed with our own, more developed reasoning abilities). We know our children are physically safe and in a safe environment, but all too often they do not actually feel or experience this safety. Instead, their mind and body sends and receives signals indicating the presence of perceived threats or danger. And sadly, for many of our kids this has become a chronic state. Until we can help our children replace their state of fear with a foundation of trust, they are likely to continue to misinterpret the safety and love that actually surrounds them.

Consider, for example, when you tell your child it is time for bed and he refuses to go and does so disrespectfully. You know it is time for bed, and you know he is going to be safe in his bed. But with our children we must always consider if what we know as reality is in fact the reality that they perceive. Does your child experience night terrors? Does going to bed and being in his room all alone trigger memories or fears, even ones he may not be able to fully articulate? Even if your child shares a room with a sibling, does going to bed create a heightened sense of loneliness? These are just some of the considerations that parents should be mindful of. Similar situations can play out around bath time, before meals, while getting ready for school, before leaving on a trip or in any number of other circumstances. Our children have a myriad of past harms and hurts, and their fear response is often activated (and remains activated). Again, many of our children simply live in a constant state of fear, not of anything specific, but as an overall state of being.

While this may be difficult to understand, if you think about it, our children are not altogether different from us when it comes to how they handle and respond to fear. After all, have you ever considered why God needed to offer the reminder to "fear not" over and over again in Scripture? And why is it that we need to be reminded so often of His presence and provision, and that we are to trust in Him rather than resorting to our own fear? He knows that He is with us, and because of His faithfulness in our lives, we should know that too. But all too often we forget. We fail to operate from a place of trust based on our relationship with our Heavenly Father. We revert instead to worry, fear and anxiety, which betray our position of security and protection as children adopted into the family of God. In spite of this, God is ever patient to lovingly remind and invite us (in ways large and small) to trade our fear for trust in Him. And it is important to notice that it is this trust that displaces fear. Even more, our children need this kind of patient and loving approach as we help them see fear for what it is, and as we help them build trust in us as the ones whom God has provided to help them heal and grow.

In combating the fear that cripples our children it is also important that parents focus on giving voice to their child. Throughout Scripture we see many people of God, including Moses, David and the prophets, expressing their doubts, fears and feelings to God. We are created to connect, and a primary way connection is achieved is through expressing ourselves to those who will listen, understand and care enough to respond. The trouble is that fear robs our children of their voice, so as parents we must be intentional about giving our children voice and restoring this essential avenue for connection. We must remember, however, that our children are not likely to find their voice on their own. Therefore, we must be intentional to give them voice (respectful and appropriate, of course) in every interaction, and in particular when we are correcting.

Questions to Consider and Discuss:

1. What triggers a fear response in your child?

2. Does your child typically respond to fear with a fight, flight or freeze response? How do you typically interpret and respond to your child's fear response?

3. Do you generally interpret these responses or behaviors as being driven by fear, or do you often interpret them as simply defiance or belligerence?

4. Thinking about it from your child's perspective, has your child experienced a lack of felt safety involving situations where you know they are "safe" but they clearly do not feel safe? Explain.

5. What kinds of behaviors have you seen in response to this? How have you handled this?

Overcoming Fear*

Question: *My son (age 6) recently had a very traumatic experience. He and his brother were swimming in the lake and playing on a small raft when a gust of wind swept through and lifted the raft out of the water, throwing him off and into the water. The water was only two to three feet deep and neither of them was injured, but they were of course very, very scared.*

I am not sure what to do now. My son told me that he is never, ever going back in the water. I know that many parents would push to get him back on the proverbial horse (and into the water) as soon as possible, but given my son's history of trauma and his struggles with fear I wonder if that is the proper approach for him. He loves the water and I don't want him to lose that joy or the great sensory feedback he gets from it. How do you recommend I help him deal with his fear?

The Empowered to Connect Team Responds: You are right in wanting your son to get back in the water soon so that he doesn't lose his love for water and lose the nurturing sensory aspects of this type of play. You are also right to be sensitive to this situation and his reaction. It can be easy to dismiss situations like this as "no big deal," but for many of our kids, with their histories and experiences, things like this are a "big deal" and will continue to be so until we have helped them work through their fears. Especially knowing how easily fear overtakes him, there are several primary types of encouragement that come to mind to help him recover from the trauma of this experience.

First, let him tell his story about what happened (over and over if necessary). Maybe even go to a family friend's swimming pool or a public pool where he feels safe, and in the course of swimming, or while sitting on the side of the pool having a snack, or an ice cream cone on the way home, let him tell the story about what happened and about his fear. We know that when children can give voice to their fears, they can begin to gain mastery over them. For many children, telling their story occurs best in the context of movement (e.g., swimming in a swimming pool, playing a card game, taking a walk, riding a bike, etc.). In addition, for many children telling their story is easier with a "distractor" (such as eating an ice cream cone or making a special snack or meal together).

Second, think about some type of "magic feather." Remember the children's story about Dumbo (the elephant with large ears who could fly)? In the story, Dumbo needed something that made him feel confident and empowered until he realized that he could in fact truly fly. As in the movie, there's no real "magic" to the "magic feather." Instead, the "magic feather" simply represents a tool to help your son address and overcome his fears. You could think of many examples of "magic feathers"—maybe a heavier raft, some type of weather alert watch or practicing a safety/escape plan—that could help to empower him and help him to feel safer and more in control. Your son may be able to help you find just the right "magic feather" that helps him regain his confidence and overcome his fear. Try asking him, "What would make you feel safer when swimming in the lake?" Sometimes just the ritual of buying a special item helps promote a sense of empowerment. It certainly helps a child feel "heard" about their pain and fear.

Third, and most important, assure him that you and/or his father are going to swim with him as long as he needs you to. Of course, this takes a great deal of intentionality and planning on your part, but it is worth it. Consider having the children hold hands between you and your husband (all the kids holding hands with a parent on each side) and walking into the water together, then staying close—as close as the children need you, for as long as they need you. Maybe you can even learn some new water games, or let them teach you their favorites; or maybe buy a few new water toys the family can play with together. By "wading back into the water" with him, you will undoubtedly help to restore his confidence and allow him to address his fears, even as it builds connections and a sense of deep trust between you (as parents) and him.

In the end, your goal is to help him overcome his fears and rediscover the joy (and therapeutic benefits) of playing and swimming in the water. Sometimes it is helpful to use "gimmicks," "gadgets," and "gizmos" as transitional aides for helping children heal, but we are always decidedly aware that these things are only bridge-making tools. The true healing for our children only comes in safe, loving relationships with insightful, nurturing and attentive parents. While we use these bridging mechanisms, the ultimate message we want our children to hear, understand and take to heart is we are there for them when they need us, in the ways they need us, for as long as they need us!

Adapted from a post on Empowered To Connect at www.empoweredtoconnect.org/resources.

Key Scripture Verses

*God is our refuge and strength,
an ever-present help in trouble.
Therefore we will not fear, though the earth give way*

and the mountains fall into the heart of the sea,
though its waters roar and foam
and the mountains quake with their surging.

—Psalm 46:1-3 (NIV)

The Bad News is Also the Good News

As we look at the challenges that our children present we must always keep in mind that the foe we are fighting against is not our children. Rather, we are fighting side-by-side with our children against the effects of their painful history and the fear that history creates. Fear is most certainly a formidable foe and the "bad news" is that in many cases our children's brains have reorganized themselves around their history and the hard places they have endured. However, the "bad news" is also the "good news"—the same malleable capacity of a child's brain to reorganize around trauma or harm also allows that child's brain to reorganize itself around felt safety and trust. This is precisely the reason that we must provide our children with the gift of trust and allow that trust to be an agent of healing and displace the fear in their lives.

As we stated previously, the past affects the future, but it does not determine it. No matter what comes our way, we must stay focused on helping our children chart a new course for the future. Together we can trade fear for trust in each other and in a God who promises to be our refuge and strength in every situation.

More Questions to Consider and Discuss:

1. What are some of your greatest fears?

2. Intellectually, what do you know about the validity of those fears in light of God's love and provision for you?

3. What helps to alleviate your fears?

4. Recognizing the role that fear is playing in your child's life, how can you best respond to help him/her exchange his/her fear for trust?

Chapter 5
Teaching Life Values

Train a child in the way he should go, and when he is old he will not turn from it.

— Proverbs 22:6 (NIV)

Part of the role of good Christian parents is undoubtedly teaching their children the values they cherish. We want our children to understand the importance of these values and, more importantly, to live a life that reflects them. Respect for others (and yourself), kindness, gentleness, self-control and other similar character qualities provide our children with a solid foundation and prepare them for the future. The question for parents, however, is how best to teach these values in ways our children can understand and make their own. Specifically, we need to ask how we can best do this for our children who come from hard places and have not had these things consistently taught, modeled or esteemed.

Teaching Your Values by Living Them First

When it comes to teaching their children values, I suspect most parents naturally think first of using words to communicate their message. Whether it is a story from a book, an everyday life experience or a passage of Scripture, many parents equate teaching with talking (and often with an air of seriousness, at that).

You've probably heard the saying that, when it comes to children, things (such as values) are better "caught" than "taught." This saying expresses the understanding that teaching is not something parents do so much as it is the sum expression of who they are in front of and with their children. As followers of Jesus Christ, Christian parents are eager to instill in their children that which they believe and hold dear. However, our children may actually learn more about our beliefs and values, and what they look like lived out, from our reaction to someone swerving in front of us on the freeway or our child spilling his drink (again), than from our talking to them about the Bible or sitting down for a "teaching moment." This truth echoes the essence of the quote often attributed to St. Francis of Assisi, "Preach the gospel at all times; use words if necessary."

Even when we do resort to traditional teaching and instruction, parents of children from hard places often discover that their children learn quite differently. As a result, we are required to take a much different approach in order to help them understand the importance of and consistently apply what we are teaching. To do this we need to be willing to dispense with protracted lectures and sermons about right and wrong and do's and don'ts as our primary means of teaching. Instead, we need to employ strategies such as short teaching scripts (i.e., role play), playful engagement and other creative approaches that can more effectively connect with our children. Our children need concrete and simple examples communicated in non-threatening ways and reinforced with lots of praise and encouragement. In addition, it is critical that these things be taught and modeled by parents who are fully present and completely attentive to their child.

Parents find that this different approach is very effective with kids from hard places. But be careful as you introduce or transition to this new way of interacting with your children because kids do say the darnedest things. One mom reminded me of this as she recounted the story of her son Grant, age five at the time, who was being mouthy and disrespectful. Choosing to engage him playfully in order to de-escalate the situation before taking advantage of the opportunity to teach him about the importance of respect, this mom lightheartedly asked him, "Where did sweet Grant go?" Without missing a beat, Grant replied, "He went on vacation and he's not coming back!" This mom certainly got her teachable moment, and then some.

Jesus Says Share!

By Dr. Karyn Purvis

There was a terrible clatter coming from the upstairs bedroom. Running swiftly up the stairs, I arrived in one of my son's bedrooms. To my great dismay, I saw my oldest son, who was generally a gentle-spirited child, with his hands around the throat of his younger brother, who was clutching a toy tightly to his chest. Shaking him angrily by the neck, my oldest son was shouting, "Jesus says share!" On the wall beside them was the Scripture I had so carefully and lovingly calligraphed for their room. Its words—"Blessed are the peacemakers ..."—seemed to mock me now. I swiftly jumped between the boys, separating them so we could resolve the conflict in a more appropriate manner. Once they settled back to play, I returned back downstairs where I reflected on what happened.

Pondering what I had witnessed, my heart grew a bit heavy. The sight of my son enlisting Jesus to his side as he choked his brother invoked more than a bit of irony and was, in a certain sense, a bit funny ... once it was all over and everyone was safe. Despite the humor I found in the situation, however, my heavy heart caused me to ask if it was possible that I had somehow "taught" my boys this attitude. Was it possible that I had succeeded in teaching them the words of God without teaching them the meaning of those words and about His very nature? In the end, I learned a lot from this single encounter—it reminded me that I must always teach my children (with my words and my actions) about how we are called to live and to love.

Key Scripture Verses

These commandments that I give you today are to be upon your hearts. Impress them on your children. Talk about them when you sit at home and when you walk along the road, when you lie down and when you get up. Tie them as symbols on your hands and bind them on your foreheads. Write them on the doorframes of your houses and on your gates.

—Deuteronomy 6:6-9 (NIV)

You Get What You Give

When it comes to this important task of teaching values to our children, parents must face a challenging reality—we are likely to get what we give. If parents want to teach their children to treat others with respect, they must first model it and live it with their children and others. I love how *The Message* phrases Moses' words from Deuteronomy 6:6-7: "Write these commandments that I've given you today on your hearts. Get them inside of you and then get them inside of your children." If we want our children to learn and live these values, then we as parents must first write them on our hearts and get them inside of us.

Countless times I've had parents tell me with obvious frustration how their child is always yelling at home and seldom shows respect. Often I will lovingly respond by asking a simple, yet pointed question: "How much yelling do you do, and do you consistently treat others in your home with respect?" I don't ask these questions to shame or point fingers, but rather to make clear an undeniable and important point that parents must always remember: *we must give to our children what we expect from them*.

Whether it is showing respect, speaking with kindness, being gentle, maintaining self-control, using calm words instead of anger or violence or any host of other important values, we are our child's primary teacher and model. The greatest lessons we will teach are not with our words, but with our actions.

A glorious custom in the days of the Old Testament was to build altars in places where God had delivered His people and made covenants with them. As people walked by the altars, they would tell the stories of old to each other and to their children. In this way, rather than sermons and lectures, one generation would pass on its stories to the next generation. These stories became poignant teachers of the family's values and history.

Likewise, as reflected in the Gospels, Jesus also preferred stories and parables as a principal means of teaching and instructing. He commonly turned to stories and examples involving nature (e.g., the lilies of the field and the birds of the air), everyday life (e.g., a farmer sowing seed or a wise man building a house) to teach, encourage and even correct others. Although He certainly knew and quoted the Hebrew Scripture, Jesus just as often resorted to stories and practical illustrations as his primary teaching tools during his ministry on earth. Most importantly, he spent time with the disciples and embodied the truths he sought to teach. Our children are fully capable of learning and living our values, but they need us to approach them with strategies that connect and meet them where they are.

Questions to Consider and Discuss:

1. Think back on your life and consider the life lessons and values that you have "caught"—those life lessons and values that you learned and have sunk in deep? Who "threw" those life lessons and values your way and how did they do it?

2. What values do you most want your child to learn and to live? How do you teach those values to your child? Do you consistently model them?

3. What are some bad habits, unhealthy tendencies or unacceptable behaviors that your child may have "inherited" from you as a parent or that you're actually modeling? What are some specific steps you can take to begin to change that?

4. What are some different strategies that you can consider using to better teach the values you want your child to learn? Look back at Chapter 5 of *The Connected Child* and the Empowered To Connect website for some specific ideas.

Chapter 6
You Are the Boss

Fathers, don't exasperate your children by coming down hard on them. Take them by the hand and lead them in the way of the Master.

— Ephesians 6:4 (*The Message*)

What if becoming the parent God has called you to be to your child from a hard place means that you need to un-learn as much or more than you need to learn? What if many of the popular approaches to parenting and discipline, many of which are regarded as "biblical," actually aren't best for your child given his background and history and what he needs to heal and grow? What if the parenting program you previously used, even with great success, when raising and training your other children needs to be significantly altered or even discarded for the child you adopted? What if the parenting techniques that most of your friends are using or that you grew up with are likely to be ineffective in achieving long-lasting change for the child you now love and desire to connect with?

I believe that parents need to seriously consider these and many similar questions as they set the course for how to best relate to and parent children from hard places. More importantly, parents need to honestly engage the question, "Am I willing to unlearn and let go of certain ways of parenting?" If you're willing, what "new things" do you need to learn and, most importantly, how do you go about doing this?

Learning to Keep Your Balance

We have come to conclude that many traditional parenting approaches and programs, including many promoted in our churches, are simply not effective for children from hard places. Many of these approaches often tend toward the extremes, while also failing to reflect the heart of God for our children. They are either overly harsh, punitive and authoritarian in nature (referred to in the child development literature as "Authoritarian Parenting") or overly permissive, excusing and lacking a healthy amount of structure (referred to as "Permissive Parenting"). Tragically, parenting styles falling within either of these extremes often serve to compound the problems they intend to address, while leaving parents and children more frustrated, disconnected and discontent.

The Balancing Act:
Parenting With Nurture & Structure

sources: Baumrind; Maccoby & Martin

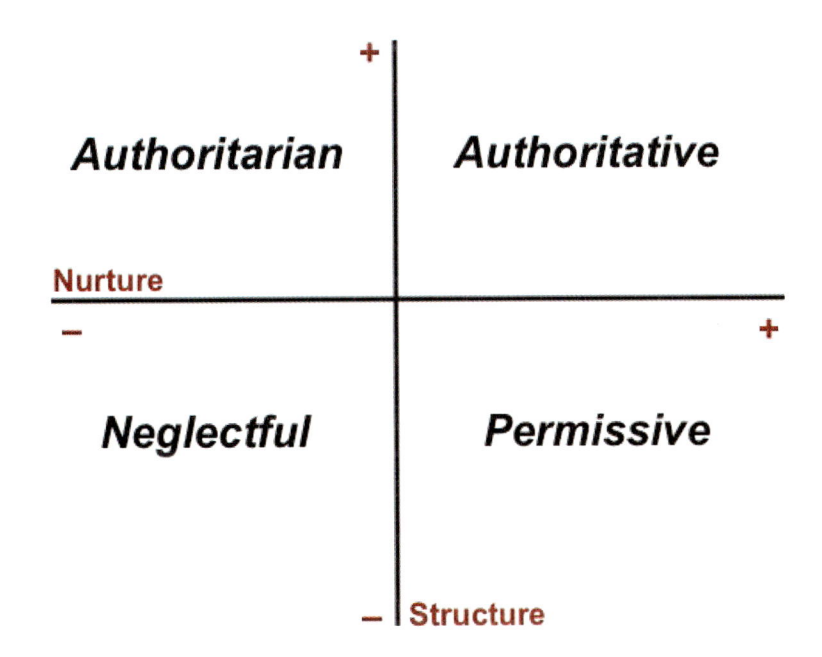

Authoritarian	**Authoritative**
Neglectful	**Permissive**

Nurture (+/−) / Structure (+/−)

    As we mentioned, many parents are inclined toward Authoritarian Parenting (located in the upper left quadrant of the above illustration) or the "law and order" approach, focusing almost exclusively on structure—rules, requirements, control, consequences and punishment. Misbehavior is met with more and more structure, with a focus on changing the behavior above all else. With this high structure, low nurture approach, every offense is met with a consequence or punishment, and as the behaviors persist or escalate so too does the punishment.

    Yet both research and experience show this approach is almost certain to fail with at-risk children. Because many of our children lack a solid foundation of trust, which ideally would've been established in the first year of life, attempts to establish authority (i.e., "who's the boss") without connection generally prove ineffective. Ironically, research indicates this reality persists even as children grow older, evidenced, for example, by the fact that children from homes with an emphasis on structure without a corresponding emphasis on nurture are more likely to engage in hard drug use and other acting out behaviors as teens.

    Conversely, other parents practice Permissive Parenting (located in the lower right quadrant of the above illustration) by focusing almost exclusively on nurture, ignoring altogether their child's need for structure to learn to regulate his behavior and develop healthy relationships. In their desire to be compassionate and extend grace to their child, these parents sacrifice the structure their child needs. This is seen in a parent who allows her child to behave in hurtful and even cruel ways because, as she said, "he has already been through so much I simply want to show him God's love and grace." One mother told us she allowed her daughter to repeatedly attack her, bruising her face and body, and accepted the beatings believing she was showing God's love to her daughter. Instead of helping their child heal and grow, however, these parents are offering "cheap grace" by allowing their child to operate without boundaries, guidance and correction. As a result, this approach also fails to bring about the lasting change parents desire, just as it does in our lives when we cheapen the grace God extends to us.

Instead, we are convinced that parents need to find a new balance in their approach to parenting, referred to as an Authoritative Parenting style (located in the upper right quadrant of the illustration on page 37). Particularly for children with difficult and painful histories, parents need to apply this balance in order to truly connect with their children and lead them toward healing and lasting connections. This balance isn't found so much in mastering the "right" parenting program (be it "Christian" or otherwise) as it is in understanding and applying the principles of Paul's instructions in Ephesians 6:4 to "take our children by the hand and lead them in the way of the Master" (*The Message*). Different translations and versions of Scripture use slightly different terms to communicate this point (including "nurture and admonition," "discipline and instruction," and "training and instruction") but the essential idea remains: as parents we are responsible for connecting with and correcting our children in a way that shows them the love of Jesus. It is in providing a consistent balance comprised of equal parts of high nurture (connecting) and high structure (correcting) that we can best lead our children in the direction they need to go and show them the love of God in tangible ways.

This conclusion is also supported by child development research that confirms that an optimal environment for children is one in which there is an equal balance between nurture and structure. This Authoritative Parenting style is rooted in the belief that the Law (structure) is our teacher and that Grace (nurture) is our guide. In fact, the research supports that those children who experience this ideal balance are at a lower risk for acting out behaviors in adolescence. The parent who understands the need for a balance of nurture and structure is most likely to be successful with the at-risk child.

I like to think of this as yet another example of science catching up with God. After all, isn't this how God relates to us as His children? Using a balance of both nurture (His tender mercies) and structure (His guiding hand that directs and corrects us), He kindly, yet firmly, leads us into a right relationship with Him. The apostle Paul puts it this way: "God is kind, but he's not soft. In kindness he takes us firmly by the hand and leads us into a radical life-change" (Romans 2:4, *The Message*). Both we and our children need love that is expressed in ways that lead to connection and transformation.

Questions to Consider and Discuss:

1. Growing up did your parents place more of an emphasis on structure or nurture, or was there a balance in your home? What influence does your experience growing up (in terms of how you were parented) have on the way you are currently parenting?

2. Overall, do you tend more toward structure or nurture in parenting your child? If you have more than one child, is your approach the same for all of your children or does it differ from child to child?

3. How do you view the way God loves and relates to you in terms of nurture and structure? Does this view of how God loves and relates to you influence the way you love and relate to your child? If so, how?

4. What are some aspects of your parenting approach that may be a little out of balance? Be specific.

Learning New Ways to Relate

As we mentioned at the beginning of this chapter, in order to engage your children with a balance of structure and nurture you may need to un-learn some of the old ways of relating to them. At the same time, you will definitely want to learn some new ways of relating to them—especially ways that are proven to be effective with children from hard places. Two important ideas that exemplify this "new way" of relating to our children are learning and applying the IDEAL response and using Re-Do's to correct misbehavior. Let's look at each more closely in the light of some real world examples.

The IDEAL acrostic is discussed in more detail in Chapter 6 of *The Connected Child*. If you are not familiar with this approach, take a few minutes to read pages 96-97 of *The Connected Child* and watch the video at http://empoweredtoconnect.org/the-ideal-response-for-parents/.

To recap, IDEAL is an acrostic that stands for:

- **I** – Immediate
- **D** – Direct
- **E** – Efficient
- **A** – Action-based
- **L** – Leveled at the behavior (not at the child)

Embedded in this simple approach to responding to misbehavior is the principle of balancing structure and nurture. When it is applied consistently by attentive and insightful parents, this aproach will yield more connection, greater contentment and the desired change in behavior, as compared to approaches that tend toward the extremes we mentioned earlier.

A Less Than IDEAL Response

By Michael & Amy Monroe

The thought of an outdoor family photo strikes fear in the hearts of most parents with young children. This experience can leave even the best parents feeling utterly powerless against both the weather and their children's behavior. The stress starts even before the picture day arrives. Finding coordinated outfits and keeping everyone's hair perfectly combed is a challenge all its own. This humbling and expensive rite of passage leaves many parents wishing for one thing above all else:

Please Lord, let them smile!

Let's face it, situations like this can bring out the worst not only in our children, but also in us as parents. This was the case during what will certainly be known for all time as the Monroe Family Picture Fiasco of 2009. But from the mess of our poor handling of the situation came a real opportunity for better understanding and a chance to learn from our mistakes.

Two Wrongs Won't Make It Right

Everything was set for the early morning photo session at a local park and everyone looked "picture perfect." The photographer started with the kids, positioning all four (ranging in age from five to nine) on a white rock in front of the beautiful waterfall. She backed away and lifted the camera to her eye ... and then it all began to fall apart.

Carter, our five-year-old boy, decided that he simply was not going to smile. There was no real reason that we could tell, he just wasn't going to. The photographer started with the old standby of silly faces. But it was to no avail. Then Mom and Dad got in on the act with a few tickles that quickly led to begging and pleading—still no smile. In fact, at that point Carter started to show more than a little attitude, as in, "I'm not smiling and you can't make me." And that's when we began to make a real mess of things.

Despite our sincere desire to be good parents we made some major mistakes in dealing with Carter's behavior. Looking back, we were primarily focused on wanting our kids to behave, not to mention wanting a good family photo. As a result, we failed to see his misbehavior as an opportunity for teaching and connection, even if it was coming at a most inopportune time. We started by using bribes, from promising candy to going swimming later that day, and when that approach didn't work we immediately moved to threats. The more he refused to cooperate, the more we threatened him. The more we threatened him, the more he refused to cooperate. We were in a battle and we weren't about to lose—not to a five-year-old. After all, we're the boss, right?

As the battle continued to escalate, Carter eventually began crying, which needless to say, doesn't portray the "happy family" we wanted everyone to see in our photos. Frustrated and embarrassed, it was time to pull out the "big guns." We took Carter aside and threatened to take away every privilege and ounce of possible fun he could imagine—*for the rest of his life*—if he did not stop crying and start cooperating by smiling NOW! These threats were accompanied by an onslaught of words, questions and accusations in increasingly louder and frustrated tones: "What is wrong with you?" "You are going to ruin this photo!" "We are wasting our money!" and "Why do you always do this?" Those are just a few of the not-so loving and kind things we said to him in our fit of frustration. But again, it was to no avail. The more we vented and raised our voices, the more Carter fell apart. By the end he was so upset that he couldn't have smiled even if he had wanted to.

Our missteps along the way were too numerous to count; our approach was anything but ideal. We tried all of the obvious and convenient tactics but they led us nowhere. To make things worse, we lost sight of what was most important. Our goal should not have been good behavior; our goal should have been (and must always be) to deepen the connection between our child and us, even— maybe especially—when we have to correct. That connection can then serve as the foundation that helps our kids make the right choices and, when they fail to, allows us to help them get back on track. Instead, we lost our focus and allowed our frustration to keep us from connecting with Carter and him with us.

Later that day we discovered, much to our shame, that Carter wasn't feeling well. He was diagnosed the next day with a major sinus infection, which is a chronic condition for him and one of several legacies of the "hard place" from which he comes. While this certainly does not excuse his misbehavior and refusal to cooperate, it does highlight the need to better understand and appreciate the complex array of factors and influences that are always present with our children. Had we chosen to handle the situation differently by spending time trying to talk (and listen) to Carter about why he wasn't cooperating and less time bribing, threatening and venting our frustrations, he likely would have told us he wasn't feeling well and we could have given him a big hug and talked with him about how we could help him feel better. If we had taken the time to respond to Carter in an IDEAL way as suggested in *The Connected Child*, seeking to connect even as we corrected, we likely could have avoided a very frustrating situation for all of us.

Back home, after all of the apologies were made (including many from us to all of the kids) and accepted and after everyone had calmed down (including Dad, who spent more than a few minutes in the "think it over" chair himself), we were able to talk about the Monroe Family Picture Fiasco of 2009 with a few laughs. As things turned out, the photos weren't all that bad. The photographer even managed to sneak a couple of great shots of Carter smiling somewhere along the way! And in the end, despite our less than ideal handling of the situation, Mom and Dad learned some valuable lessons, and we all grew a little closer together as a family.

Key Scripture Verses

When they landed, they saw a fire of burning coals there with fish on it, and some bread. When they had finished eating, Jesus said to Simon Peter, "Simon son of John, do you truly love me more than these?"

   "Yes, Lord," he said, "you know that I love you."

   Jesus said, "Feed my lambs."

Again Jesus said, "Simon son of John, do you truly love me?"

   He answered, "Yes, Lord, you know that I love you."

   Jesus said, "Take care of my sheep."

The third time he said to him, "Simon son of John, do you love me?"

   Peter was hurt because Jesus asked him the third time, "Do you love me?" He said, "Lord, you know all things; you know that I love you."

   Jesus said, "Feed my sheep."

—John 21:9, 15-17 (NIV)

Another Chance to Get it Right

Scripture records only two accounts of a charcoal fire, yet these accounts tell two very different aspects of a single story that is particularly instructive for us as both followers of Christ and as parents. Both accounts are found in John's Gospel (Chapters 18 and 21), and they bookend one of the most well known interactions between Jesus and the apostle Peter. The first account involves Peter's denial of Jesus just before his death; the second records Jesus' restoration of Peter following his resurrection.

Peter surely represents one of the most memorable figures among all of Jesus' disciples. Impulsive, self-assured and outspoken, Peter was never one to hold back. We see this as Peter jumps to Jesus' defense in the garden the night before his crucifixion. Likewise, in response to Jesus' prediction that Peter would deny him, we find Peter unwavering in his insistence that he would never do such a thing. But only a short time later, Peter is standing in the temple courtyard warming himself around a charcoal fire (John 18:18) and, when asked whether he is associated with this Jesus who is about to be crucified, Peter denies Jesus not once, but three times, confirming his denial with an oath.

Few accounts in all of the Gospels so vividly evidence our human condition of sin and weakness. And yet, shortly after the resurrection, Jesus encounters Peter—again around a charcoal fire—and fully restores him (John 21). We see this complete restoration on display in Peter's response to Jesus asking him for a third time, "Do you love me?" (John 21:17), when Peter answers by relying on Jesus' knowledge of Peter's own heart. Surely this is the ultimate of connections—to understand that we are fully known and fully loved by Jesus.

This passage in John 21 is a beautiful example of Jesus giving Peter an opportunity to "return to the scene of his crime" and "try it again." There, beside the charcoal fire, Jesus offered Peter a chance to get it right—a "re-do" of sorts—by professing his love for the Master. It serves as a great model for us as followers of Christ and as parents. The location and manner in which Jesus offered Peter a "re-do" were not accidents. Likewise, we as parents should be just as intentional in offering our children opportunities like this as often as we can. Giving our children the chance to "try it again" and get it right is an effective way to correct behavior, particularly for less serious behaviors. In addition, this approach provides them with "motor memory" for doing the right thing and offers an opportunity for us to give praise and encouragement once they re-do the task or follow the instruction. These outcomes help our children experience doing the right thing and help to deepen our connections with them as well.

Questions to Consider and Discuss:

1. Think back to a recent example of when your child misbehaved and you handled the situation less than ideally. Applying the IDEAL approach, what could you have done differently in that situation?

2. In what ways has God offered you a "re-do" when you've sinned and missed the mark?

3. Why is it sometimes difficult to offer your child a "re-do"?

4. What behaviors does your child exhibit that might be best responded to with a "re-do"? Pick one or two and discuss in detail how you would go about using this strategy.

CHAPTER 7
Dealing with Defiance

Children, obey your parents in the Lord, for this is right.

— Ephesians 6:1 (NIV)

In working with parents from all over, we have observed one thing that stretches them to the breaking point more than any other: *outright defiance*. Parents are generally open and willing to consider many of the principles and approaches explained in *The Connected Child*, and many parents are eager to embrace the holistic approach that we advocate as they focus on making connections and building trust. They are willing to focus on nurture, look for opportunities to playfully engage their child and consider their child's history and complex needs when assessing and dealing with behaviors. But in the face of open defiance—what parents clearly see as willful disobedience and outright disrespect—their blood begins to boil and their "law and order" instincts kick in.

This reaction is certainly understandable, and we would be the last ones to suggest that your child should be allowed to be disobedient, disrespectful or defiant without correction. However, the real heart of the matter is not *if* you correct defiance and disobedience but *how* you correct it.

Is It Adoption or Not?

Closely related to the issue of dealing with defiance is the question that all adoptive parents have asked themselves at some point—*is it adoption-related or not?* When a child with a difficult history (or perhaps a history that is largely unknown) is disrespectful, starts acting up, has frequent meltdowns, is out of control or even becomes violent, it is understandable for parents to wonder whether, and to what extent, the behaviors are related to the child's history or are simply "normal" (albeit unacceptable) behaviors for a child of that age.

As important and as valid as that question may seem, asking, "Is it adoption-related or not?" often doesn't lead us in a helpful direction. In fact, the question can cause parents to get sidetracked in their attempt to stay focused on responding in the best possible way. That is not to say that we shouldn't have compassion for our child's history (we must), nor is it to say that our child's history does not affect behavior (it does). Ultimately, the answer to the question, "Is this behavior adoption-related or not?" may always remain something of an unknown. Yet, given all that we know from the ever-growing body of research, the answer to the question is almost always, at least in part, "yes." So in the end where does that leave us?

We are convinced that the principles that must guide and shape the way you relate and respond to your child should not change, regardless of whether the behavior you are addressing is presumed to be adoption or foster care-related or not. After all, the relationship with your child is what you should remain focused on, so building trust and strengthening connections with your child should always be the foundation for addressing behaviors in ways that effectively correct.

Staying Focused on Connecting Even When Correcting

To be clear, our approach should *never* be understood to endorse parents permitting or ignoring defiance. I often tell parents that I am "zero tolerance" when it comes to disrespect and other forms of defiance. Although the word "defiance" does not appear in Scripture, there are plenty of examples of it, starting in the Garden of Eden. God does not accept, ignore or look past defiance, and as parents, neither should we.

At the same time, it is important to note that Scripture does not reveal a "one size fits all" approach to correcting a child's defiance or disobedience even though there is no shortage of books claiming to offer *the* biblical way to parent and discipline. We must keep in mind that not tolerating defiance does not mean that we must always come down hard or forcefully on our kids. Taking a "zero tolerance" approach in dealing with defiance does not excuse us to abandon our efforts at connecting and building trust with our children, especially when they need correcting. To the contrary, both research and experience indicate that it is imperative that parents of children from hard places consistently seek to connect, even when correcting.

When our children are defiant or disobedient, it's important that our response be efficient. There is a great deal of literature about the importance and efficacy of parents using an appropriate or measured level of response to correct misbehavior. Many parents mistakenly believe that an all-out nuclear assault is the only right response to defiant behavior. For example, I've heard of small children losing privileges for several weeks for refusing to go straight to bed when told to do so. These parents fear that if they give an inch their child will take a mile, and so they feel compelled to act swiftly, decisively and often harshly. In fact, some parenting approaches strongly criticize attempts to have the punishment "fit the crime," and instead advocate that parents respond with a punishment that is both punitive and painful (be it physical or otherwise). These approaches suggest that harsh punishments are the only way to make an impression on a child and will make the child less likely to repeat the defiant or disobedient behavior.

While there is a certain logic to this mindset, it ignores a number of important realities for our children, not the least of which is their history and their propensity to live and operate in a constant state of fear. As we explained in Chapter 4, most of our children still desperately need to replace fear with trust, and until they do, logic and consequence-based approaches are likely to make matters worse, not better.

Instead, thinking back to Chapter 6, you will recall that as part of the IDEAL response we advocate that parents respond immediately (that is the "I" in IDEAL). But equally important is that parents act efficiently (that is the "E" in IDEAL). An efficient response is one that uses only the amount of correction needed to address the behavior and "get the train back on the track." And again, during and after situations that require correction, we believe it is critical for the emphasis to remain on maintaining (and even strengthening) our connection to our children.

Does Defiance Always Require a Serious Response?

Some parents find themselves perplexed when it comes to dealing with defiance and other misbehavior. Instinctively, they know it is "serious business." They know it is not right or good (and certainly not pleasing to the Lord) for their children to be defiant or disobedient. Because parents love their children, they know that they must respond to misbehavior. However, many parents automatically conclude that they're required to respond in a very serious and authoritative manner. As a result, parents instinctively resort to the "big voice," start the countdowns (you can hear it now: "one … two … two and a half …"), threaten punishments or consequences, take privileges away and on and on. These responses are levied against virtually every infraction, be it large or small.

But there are other practical ways to connect while correcting that allow parents to treat defiance as serious business without requiring them to always be so, well, serious. One key strategy is to use playful engagement in correcting interactions with your child whenever possible. In the face of defiant behavior, playful engagement is an approach proven to be very effective for children from hard places. Even when a situation requires that you actually become more "serious" in order to stop and correct a behavior (for example, by using a firm tone, louder volume and slower cadence in your voice, or by communicating you mean business with your facial expression and posture), it is important to return to playful engagement as quickly as possible once the situation is over and the behavior is changed or corrected.

Making the Right Moves in the Defiance Battle

By Amy Monroe

Susan recently recounted a recurring issue she was dealing with at home with her six-year-old son, Seth, whom she adopted from foster care. The situation was becoming increasingly problematic and was causing a great deal of frustration. It involved outright defiance, but it started with a simple pair of socks.

Getting ready for school can be a challenging undertaking. Kids are cranky, parents are rushed—the whole routine is a recipe for disaster. While getting ready for school, Susan asked Seth to give her his socks so she could help him put them on. Somewhat playfully (but also to push her buttons), Seth threw the socks toward her. Following the advice of the therapist that her adoption agency referred, Susan immediately placed Seth in time out for six minutes (the number of minutes that matched Seth's age). The therapist also instructed that if Seth did not act appropriately while sitting in time out, Susan was to add another six minutes for each instance of misbehavior.

The morning that Seth threw the socks he ended up sitting in time out for more than 40 minutes! The next morning, he sat in time out nearly as long. Susan readily acknowledged the harm Seth had suffered in the past and that developmentally he was not yet as capable as his age might suggest. But she was equally convinced that Seth knew what he was doing and knew that it was wrong. He was being defiant and, according to what she had been told, it was imperative that she put an end to it.

After several days of this type behavior (at different times during the day), Susan finally called another mom in the adoption ministry at her church to get her take on the problem. This other mom suggested the possibility that the punishment Susan was imposing didn't really "fit the crime," and although Seth certainly should not be allowed to be defiant, there may be a more effective way to remedy the situation.

Her suggestion for Susan was simple and straight from *The Connected Child*. She suggested that Susan use playful engagement and "re-do's" in response to Seth's sock-throwing defiance (and similar infractions). Rather than treat it as a capital offense, this mom encouraged Susan to simply allow Seth to "try it again" while using a playful tone and cadence in her voice and a non-threatening posture. Ignoring the advice she had been given by the therapist regarding time outs, Susan began responding to sock throwing incidents and other situations with as much playful engagement as the situation would allow. She began offering Seth a chance to "try it again" while keeping the mood as playful as possible, but without allowing any misbehavior to go uncorrected. She was immediately encouraged by the results.

Of course, this approach didn't work immediately on every occasion. Sometimes, Seth would have to "try it again" a few times before he got it right. But all in all, Susan found this to be a far more successful approach. What's more, dealing with Seth's defiance in this manner didn't lead to frequent escalation and prolonged battles like before.

Although playfully engaging and offering "try it again" opportunities was time consuming in its own right, Susan wasn't as frustrated and drained as she was before. Not all acts of defiance are created equal and certainly no one response is right for all situations. But it is important for parents to remember what Susan discovered—although defiance and misbehavior are serious business, our response can become an avenue to deeper, more joyful connection.

Key Scripture Verses

There is a story in the Bible that offers some helpful insight into how Jesus responded to a man whose life, and indeed his very livelihood, was blatantly defiant and contrary to what God desires. His name was Zacchaeus, and Luke records Jesus' encounter with him as follows:

A man was there by the name of Zacchaeus; he was a chief tax collector and was wealthy. He wanted to see who Jesus was, but being a short man he could not, because of the crowd. So he ran ahead and climbed a sycamore-fig tree to see him, since Jesus was coming that way.

When Jesus reached the spot, he looked up and said to him, "Zacchaeus, come down immediately. I must stay at your house today." So he came down at once and welcomed him gladly.

All the people saw this and began to mutter, "He has gone to be the guest of a 'sinner.'"

But Zacchaeus stood up and said to the Lord, "Look, Lord! Here and now I give half of my possessions to the poor, and if I have cheated anybody out of anything, I will pay back four times the amount."

Jesus said to him, "Today salvation has come to this house, because this man, too, is a son of Abraham. For the Son of Man came to seek and to save what was lost."

—Luke 19:2-10 (NIV)

Relationship is the Key to Transformation

We can all probably recall the Sunday school song about Zacchaeus, but that "wee little man" and his encounter with Jesus reveals an important lesson. It is interesting to notice that Jesus, upon calling Zacchaeus down from the tree, did not rip into him with a long lecture or sermon about what a scoundrel and cheat he was. Neither did Jesus isolate him, shame him or try to punish or make an example of him. Instead, Jesus invited Zacchaeus into relationship. Sharing a meal with someone in the first century had far-reaching and profound social implications, and Jesus doing so with Zacchaeus the tax collector was nothing less than scandalous. But as with many other life-changing encounters that people had with Jesus, we see that Jesus found it important to connect with Zacchaeus in order to lead him toward transformation. No doubt this did not sit well with many, including the religious elite of that day. And if we are honest, this may not sit all that well with us as we apply it to our children. But it is difficult to read the Gospels or think about our own transforming encounter with Jesus and deny that he uses a relationship (connection) to bring about real and lasting change in response to our sin (defiance).

Likewise, parents with children from hard places are likely to encounter others who will not understand or agree with an approach that places such a significant emphasis on connecting, especially in response to defiance. Many people may misinterpret or misunderstand what we are suggesting, especially if they are not familiar with children from hard places and the impacts their histories can have. Even so, we encourage you to always remember *your* goal—to develop a deep and lasting connection with *your* child in order to help him heal and grow. Much will be required of your child along the way; even more will be required of you. In the end, however, it will be from a strong and secure foundation of connection that you will best be able to teach, correct and truly love your child.

Rules of Connected Families
(from The Connected Child, *page 136)*

- **A child** may not dominate the family through tantrums, aggression, back talk, whining or any other tactic.
- **Parents** are kind, fair and consistent; they stay calm and in control. They administer structure and limits, but they also provide a great deal of nurturing, praise and affection.
- **A child** is encouraged to use words to express his or her needs directly and respectfully.
- **Parents** honor a child's boundaries and respectfully listen to his or her needs and requests. They never shame or ridicule a child's perspective.
- **Parents** meet all reasonable needs and requests. They say, "Yes," whenever they can. Occasionally they allow a compromise, and at times they say, "No," and deny requests.
- **Parents** respond to misbehavior immediately. They redirect the child to better choices, let him or her practice getting it right and then praise their child for improvement. Once the conflict is resolved, they return to playful and warm interactions with their child.

Questions to Consider and Discuss:

1. When your child is being defiant or deliberately disobedient, what goal(s) do you hope to achieve with your response? Be specific.

2. Do you find that you sometimes "overreact" to defiance and similar misbehavior? If so, why?

3. Are you afraid that if you use playful engagement in your approach to correcting, your child (or others) will see you as a "weak" or "permissive" parent? Are you afraid this approach will not work with your child? Explain.

4. Do you think Jesus was "tough enough" in his handling of Zacchaeus?

5. Are you afraid of what others may think or say about the way you parent if you handle certain situations, especially those involving discipline, differently than they recommend? Why?

6. What are some ways you can show "zero tolerance" in your response to your child's defiance or similar misbehavior while still remaining focused on connecting? Talk about specific examples or situations.

Chapter 8
Nurturing at Every Opportunity

For God so loved the world that He gave His one and only Son ...

— John 3:16 (NIV)

God's ultimate response to sinful humanity is love—a love that gave and always gives. As Paul wrote to the Romans, "God demonstrates his own love for us in this: While we were still sinners, Christ died for us" (Romans 5:8, NIV). As those who have received this gift of undeserved love, our hope should be to demonstrate this same kind of giving, selfless love in ways that draw our children into a deeper personal relationship with our giving Lord and with us.

As parents, we have the opportunity not only to teach but to embody God's love for our children. Consider a parent tenderly cradling her newborn. The mother's face is glowing as her child peers through blurry vision to see his preciousness reflected in her joyful smile. Her voice is warm and welcoming, inviting a deep and soothing connection. A warm sensory bath of loving care envelops the infant. This scene is repeated hundreds of times in the first days of life. Out of this spontaneous, affectionate, connected dance between parent and child, this little one develops trust in the knowledge that his parent truly cares for him. In these arms of nurturing love, this child learns who he is, the meaning of unconditional love and his heart is being prepared to understand the eternal love of God.

Yet because of their histories, many of our children are not able to readily understand and accept this love because they have never come to realize just how precious they are to God and us. Many of them did not receive positive attention and healthy affection when they were young. As infants they may not have been held in the arms of adoring parents whose faces reflected an undeniable joy at the very presence of their lives. As toddlers they may have been denied nurture and comfort. As they grew older they may never have experienced affirmation, praise or encouragement.

Nurturing Guidance

Our God is a nurturing God. We see this throughout Scripture as He nurtures His children in many different ways—by comforting those who are hurting and troubled (2 Corinthians 1:3-4), by providing for our physical needs (Matthew 6:28-34), by encouraging us (Romans 15:4) and by correcting us (Hebrews 12:4-11). Yes, God nurtures even when He is correcting us.

Likewise, purposing to embody God's love to our children doesn't mean that we won't have to discipline and correct. As we've already learned, we will inhibit our children's ability to grow and develop if we do not provide the consistent correction they need. However, our correction must always be based on and flow from our relationship with and love for them, just as God's correction of us flows from His love for and relationship with us (Hebrews 12:6). In that sense we must always be connecting even when we are correcting. It is most certainly that love—from us and ultimately from God—and all that flows from it that will bring about the ultimate transformation we desire for our children.

The Power of Encouragement

I've often wondered what it would have been like to travel with the Apostle Paul on his early missionary journeys. There is no doubt that Paul was an intelligent and passionate follower of Christ whom God used mightily to shape the early church as well as to inform much of our theology. But it's also quite possible that he was more than a little exacting and probably not always very encouraging. We see a glimpse of this in his interaction with John Mark in Acts 15 where we find him less than encouraging to the young disciple.

We read in Acts 15 that Paul had become upset with John Mark because he had deserted them earlier in the journey. As a result, Paul was unwilling to suffer John Mark and his failures any longer and essentially expelled him from the team. However, Barnabas immediately stepped forward to pick John Mark up, so to speak, and to encourage him onward. After all, what would you expect from Barnabas, a man whose name meant "Son of Encouragement"?

True to the meaning of his name, Barnabas' encouragement was obviously effective as we see John Mark, also known as Mark, continue in the faith and eventually record the first written account of Jesus' ministry in the Gospel of Mark. Barnabas was able to see potential and value in John Mark that Paul simply was not able or willing to see. However, the success of Barnabas' continued encouragement and investment in John Mark was eventually recognized even by Paul himself late in his ministry when he wrote approvingly of Mark to Timothy (2 Timothy 4:11).

The reality is that we as parents of children from hard places need to always be mindful to be a 'Barnabas-like' presence in the lives of our children. There is little doubt that they will stumble, fall and fail, but the power of our encouragement, praise and affirmation should never be underestimated as we seek to help them get back on track and move forward to reach their God-given potential. Much like Barnabas did for John Mark, we must understand that our children need nurture expressed in ways that encourage and motivate them, and we must be willing to provide it as often as it is needed.

Closing the Gap

By Amy Monroe

Sue and Ron had three biological children who were healthy, happy and loved the Lord. Life was good and honestly it was fairly simple, at least until they went on a mission trip and visited a Russian orphanage. It was there that they knew in their hearts God was calling them to adopt—and not just adopt any child but a 10-year-old girl named Sasha. They were excited about what God was going to do in and through their family, but they were quite nervous as well.

Sue and Ron knew many families who had already adopted and some of what they knew about these families' experiences was more than a little scary. Most of them adopted older children from Russian orphanages, some from Sasha's orphanage, and most had encountered significant challenges not long after they returned home. As they reflected on the struggles that these families faced, Sue and Ron were determined to learn from these families' experiences.

One common aspect they observed among these families applied directly to their situation. It seemed that many of the families that adopted were already parenting biological children and doing so quite successfully overall. However, few of them were meeting with similar success in terms of applying their same parenting approach with the child they had just welcomed home. Time and time again these parents discovered that trying to fit their adopted children into the already existing patterns of life and way of doing things only resulted in heartache and frustration for everyone.

As Sue and Ron learned more about children who come from orphanage environments—the impact of their histories and what they need in order to heal—they discovered that many children who have experienced trauma and institutionalization function at an overall developmental age equal to roughly half their chronological age. For them, this meant that although Sasha would be coming home as a 10-year-old girl, she was likely to be significantly less than 10-years-old in terms of her developmental and emotional maturity. And once Sasha was home Sue and Ron immediately found this to be the case.

The truth was that Sasha had no idea what it meant to be part of a family. She had no healthy experiences giving or receiving nurture, no practice at making choices or using her words to communicate her feelings or needs and no understanding of how to control her own behavior. In addition to being aware of these realities, Ron and Sue also had some understanding about the potential impact that the years of orphanage life likely had on Sasha's physical, cognitive and emotional development.

As a result Sue and Ron committed to dramatically simplify their lives in order to provide Sasha what she needed most. They withdrew from many family outings and activities for a while—even from the routine of going to church each week, although they stayed closely connected to those in their church. They educated Sasha at home for over six months and constantly encouraged her as she learned English and tackled new academic subjects. Most importantly, they began to teach Sasha about God's love for her and to model that in practical and tangible ways.

Despite these and other efforts, Sasha seemingly could not get enough of the nurture Sue and Ron were offering. Sue found that Sasha would literally follow her around the house all day long for weeks on end. For months Sue never had any alone time until the kids had all gone to sleep. When Sasha would become upset and hysterical, often over the smallest thing, they found that holding her and even rocking her would usually help calm her. It certainly felt a bit strange to hold and rock a 10-year-old, but Sasha clearly needed the nurture. So, they did not hesitate to provide it. They affirmed Sasha consistently and praised and encouraged her at every opportunity. They allowed her to play with toys and watch television shows more suited for a 5-year-old than a girl Sasha's age. In short, they did the best they could to allow Sasha to start at the beginning and experience all that she had missed in order to connect and help develop trust.

Day by day Sue and Ron began to see significant changes in Sasha. Her confidence grew, and she was connecting with them as well as her new siblings. As they began to venture out, Sasha even began to make friends. In time, they saw the gap between Sasha's chronological and developmental age close dramatically, and they had the privilege of watching her mature and blossom into a wonderful young woman. Sue and Ron would be the first to tell you that Sasha's first year home was the most difficult year of their lives, but they would not hesitate to tell you that all of their efforts to offer Sasha the nurture she needed were more than worth the sacrifice.

Key Scripture Verses

This is my command: Love one another the way I loved you. This is the very best way to love. Put your life on the line for your friends.

—John 15:12-13 (*The Message*)

The High Cost of Love

There is a difficult truth that we must be willing to face if we are serious about loving our children the way that God would have us love them and the way they need to be loved. That truth is that biblical love is costly—very costly. In fact, it is a call to die to ourselves, and we should not pretend that it will be easy or even come naturally. God demonstrated His love for us by giving nothing less than His Son (John 3:16), and He has called us to live a life of love by giving ourselves. We have been called to love as He has loved us (John 15:12).

While this focus on love and providing nurture sounds good and right, we must be prepared for the real tensions and challenges that will undoubtedly arise. Each of us must be willing to count the cost when following Jesus (Luke 14:28) and traveling the adoption journey in a way that offers healing to our children and brings glory to our Lord. The daily decisions to be selfless rather than selfish; the constant battle between our willingness to pay the high cost of providing the love and nurture our children need versus defaulting to the convenience, ease and familiarity of simply "making them obey"—these are but a few examples of how we must choose to love, and to live out that love in ways that build trust and bring healing to our children.

It is a high calling with a high cost, but it is what He has called us to, and we dare not travel this journey on our own. God has given us His love, His Word and His Spirit to show us the way and to empower us to put our "lives of love" on the line for our children.

Questions to Consider and Discuss:

1. **Do you see yourself as a nurturing parent? Explain why or why not.**

2. How specifically can you begin to more intentionally nurture your child? How do you think he/she will respond?

3. In what ways does your child need to be nurtured (according to your child's developmental age not his/her chronological age) that you are not comfortable with or equipped to provide?

4. Thinking about how to nurture your child in terms of offering praise and encouragement, how can you specifically be more "Barnabas-like" toward your child?

5. What are some ways that you need to "put your life on the line" for your child?

CHAPTER 9
Proactive Strategies to Make Life Easier

It's in Christ that we find out who we are and what we are living for. Long before we first heard of Christ and got our hopes up, he had his eye on us, had designs on us for glorious living, part of the overall purpose he is working out in everything and everyone.

— Ephesians 1:11-12 (*The Message*)

Our God is purposeful. From before the beginning of time, He's had an "overall purpose he is working out in everything and everyone" (Ephesians 1:12, *The Message*). Even before Adam and Eve first sinned, God had a plan for our redemption. Throughout the Old Testament we read of God's preparation that would reveal, in the fullness of time, His plan for the redemption of this fallen world.

In every facet from creation forward, God has a plan, and He is always prepared and at work to accomplish it for His good pleasure. We see this in the beginning as God spoke creation into existence. My childhood pastor used to whimsically quip: "You don't see God creating fish on the first day and saying 'Hey guys, if you will just flop around on dry ground until the third or fourth day, I promise that I will get around to making water.'" No, even when we don't see it or cannot understand it, we are assured that our God has a plan, and He will accomplish it.

Preparing for the Challenges

One of my favorite examples of this from Scripture is the story of Esther. The book of Esther not only reminds us of God's plan and provision for the Jews, it offers practical tools for us today as well.

In the face of an evil plot by Haman to annihilate the Jews, Queen Esther, herself an orphan adopted by her cousin Mordecai, bravely stepped forward and overcame her fears to save her people. Although God is never mentioned in the book of Esther, we clearly see His hand at work in the lives of both Esther and Mordecai. Esther didn't sit back or shirk from the difficult and even dangerous task before her. Instead, she realized that God had placed her in a position of influence and given her a purpose for "such a time as this." She realized that she needed to be courageous, faithful and proactive in order to be used by God to accomplish that purpose. Esther was faced with a true life or death situation. Rather than ignoring the situation, waiting for someone else to step in and solve it or simply hoping that it would go away, she took initiative and employed a proactive approach. Based on the account of her step-by-step approach in persuading King Xerxes (Esther 5-7) to reverse the edict to kill all Jews, it is clear that not only was Esther proactive, she was determined and courageous.

In the face of the repeated and persistent challenges that we face with our children, we would do well to follow Esther's lead in both being proactive and preparing to meet and, as often as possible, prevent such challenges, even as we rely on the guiding hand and provision of God. Many of us know all too well those situations, places and activities that trigger our children. Knowing this, we and our children would be well served if we intentionally take practical steps to help our children better navigate these environments and avoid the typical fallout. Some of these practical steps are detailed in Chapter 9 of *The Connected Child*, and they include anticipating and managing transitions and separation, establishing choices ahead of time, watching for signs of overload and practicing how to interact with strangers, just to name a few.

Setting Our Children Up to Succeed

Despite our best efforts, our children will make mistakes and wrong choices, which will certainly provide for great teaching moments; however, acknowledging this reality is far different from "allowing" them to fail or setting them up to do so simply to create a teaching moment. We must recognize that too many children from hard places are overwhelmed by a deep sense of shame and feel as if they are hopeless, worthless and beyond help. They are keenly aware of their many failures and faults, have come to expect that they will fail and believe that we expect the same. As a result, they often oblige by meeting their own low expectations. And considering that many of them experience deeply held feelings of rejection, inadequacy and low self-worth, it is clear that our children need us to be consistently cheering for their success and setting them up to succeed as much as we possibly can. We need to understand that this is undoubtedly a significant responsibility of all parents of children from hard places.

We believe this approach also clearly reflects the heart of God. In the book of James we read that God cannot be tempted by evil, nor does He tempt us to do evil (James 1:13). Simply put, God never sets us up for moral failure even though He is not shy about using our failures and faults as teaching moments. With this in mind it is important that parents avoid the trap of 'lying in wait' for their children to fail in order to teach them a lesson. Our kids will stumble and fall frequently thereby providing us with ample opportunities to correct, teach and forgive. The truth is that we as parents will do the same, providing our Heavenly Father with no shortage of opportunities to correct, teach and forgive us. Just as God does with His children, we need to proactively plan and prepare to help our children succeed, and we need to be sure to praise them when they do.

Setting the Temperature for My Child

By Amy Monroe

I still vividly remember the battles we used to wage with one of our sons. Had we known then what we know now, our initial approach and the early outcomes would have been so very different.

This particular son deals with a significant amount of anxiety and worry. By nature he is somewhat of an introvert, but for as long as I can recall he has also been a highly anxious child. We've seen this anxiety manifest itself in many different ways, often affecting his behavior significantly and trapping him in a maze of fear and worry. What we've also come to learn is that there was much more going on in his little body than merely anxiety.

A simple example of this is that for many years he resisted transitioning from long sleeve shirts to short sleeve shirts and then back again as the seasons and temperatures changed. This may not seem like a big deal, but when your child insists on wearing long sleeves with shorts and flip-flops in the 100 degree heat of July, it begins to create some issues. Not recognizing this and similar situations for what they were—a sensory processing issue coupled with more than a little desire for control—we, like many parents, treated this behavior as straight forward stubbornness and defiance. We attempted to change his resistance first by reasoning and bargaining with him. When that failed we quickly moved to lectures, threats and imposing consequences. Rather than achieving any meaningful change, however, all we managed to do was increase his anxiety and physical discomfort as well as our frustration.

Another issue that he's consistently struggled with (even to this day) is the fear of being left or forgotten. Again, this may seem rather insignificant, but when it begins to dominate your family's planning for every outing (school, church, parties, piano practice, etc.) and causes major anxiety and leads to serious meltdowns, it is no longer insignificant. Our son would be the first to tell you that we have never left him, but even though he had no real basis for his fear, the fear was nonetheless very real to him. No amount of explaining or lecturing him about how we would never leave or forget him seemed to have any effect. The fact of the matter was that he did not feel safe and that lack of felt safety was paralyzing him and threatening to do the same to us.

After reading *The Connected Child* and talking with other parents who were facing similar situations, we realized that we hadn't been setting our son up to succeed—and not only in these areas. The reality is that we had allowed him to set the direction and as a result we kept following him head-long into challenge after challenge. Thinking about it in different terms, we had relegated our role as parents to being a thermometer of sorts—merely reflecting the temperature that he (with his anxiety and other issues) was setting—rather than being a thermostat and regulating what the temperature should be.

It was clearly time for us to become far more intentional and proactive to help our son learn how to better handle these and other situations, and to bring more joy back to our day-to-day experience with him. We approached the next change of season quite differently. Well before the upcoming season arrived we calmly talked with him about how we all would be changing the type of clothes we would be wearing. We also asked him to try to explain to us why he didn't want to wear certain shirts. As we helped him search for the right words to explain what he was experiencing we discovered some not so insignificant sensory issues such as the tags in many of his shirts made him very uncomfortable—something that can be fixed quite easily with a pair of scissors. What's more, as we patiently and calmly listened to him on this issue he began to express himself more clearly on other subjects as well. And as we began to establish choices for him ahead of time (such as "today you can wear your long sleeve shirt until lunch but when we go to the park to play I would like you to choose one of these two short sleeve shirts or tank tops to wear") we met with far less resistance to change.

As for the fears relating to being left behind, we began to be far more intentional about helping him know exactly what was going to happen in advance. We established regular pick up locations and times, and we moved heaven and earth to be sure that we were consistently in the right place at the right time. We helped create more consistency in our routines and helped him anticipate transitions throughout each day by doing small things such as taking the initiative to "check in" with him every 15 minutes while he was playing in the backyard or buying him a digital watch to wear so he would know what time we would be there to pick him up.

After several months of being intentional, proactive and consistent we began to see many of his fears dissipate. These and other steps created more predictability for him and allowed us to help set the temperature for him, rather than merely reflecting and reacting to whatever temperature he might set. In addition, this approach enabled us to develop more understanding, compassion and genuine empathy for him as we have seen him confront and in many ways overcome his anxiety. While we still have many challenges yet to conquer, I am confident that with us setting the temperature we are on the right track.

Key Scripture Verses

As Jesus concluded the Sermon on the Mount (Matthew 5-7) he offered important instruction to his listeners (and to us) about how to apply all that he had taught them.

"Therefore everyone who hears these words of mine and puts them into practice is like a wise man who built his house on the rock. The rain came down, the streams rose, and the winds blew and beat against that house; yet it did not fall, because it had its foundation on the rock. But everyone who hears these words of mine and does not put them into practice is like a foolish man who built his house on sand. The rain came down, the streams rose, and the winds blew and beat against that house, and it fell with a great crash."

—Matthew 7:24-27 (NIV)

Building a Solid Foundation

Many adoptive and foster parents have learned from experience that while there are certainly blessings and joys that mark the journey, it also comes with more than a few challenges, disappointments and heartaches along the way. In light of this undeniable reality, being proactive and prepared is really not an option for those parents who are committed to doing all they can to help their children heal and flourish. Of course there are no guarantees in life or in the adoption or foster care journey, other than the assurance that God will never leave or forsake us and that our faithfulness is not in vain.

With this in mind, being intentional, proactive and prepared to set our children up for success are key elements for building a strong foundation. It is critical that we not think of building connections, developing trust and all of the strategies that we advocate merely as tools used for responding to problems or misbehavior. After all, thinking in terms of the passage from Matthew 7:24-27, what we are building is a house in which we want to live—or in our case, a relationship with our children that is warm and joyful—not a storm shelter. Therefore, parents must spend even more time implementing this approach and employing these tools in proactive and preventative ways. Otherwise, we run the risk of being like the man that Jesus spoke of at the end of Matthew 7—building our relationship with our children on a shaky foundation because we have failed to act based on all that we have learned. Just as Jesus taught that our ultimate foundation is God's Word put into action, we as parents must act on the insights and tools we have been provided in order to build a solid foundation for our children.

As we travel the adoption journey and live out the call that God has given us we know that at times the rains will come, the streams will rise and the winds will blow against us and our children. Nevertheless, we know that God is with us in the midst of these challenges and trials, and that He is at work for our good (Romans 8:28). This is why we can, as James 1:2 says, "consider it pure joy whenever [we] face trials of many kinds," because we know that God is not only doing a good work through us, He is doing a good work in us as well. An important part of this good work in our journey is learning to be proactive and intentional as we help our children overcome their past and establish a solid foundation for a more hope-filled future.

Questions to Consider and Discuss:

1. In what areas of your parenting do you feel unprepared or lacking an adequate plan?

2. In what ways have you set your child up to succeed? In what ways have you intentionally or inadvertently set your child up to fail?

3. Does your child expect himself/herself to fail much of the time? Does your child believe that you expect him/her to fail at certain things? How can you go about changing both your and his/her expectations?

4. What are some specific ways that you can become more proactive, intentional or prepared in terms of parenting your child and setting him/her up to succeed?

Chapter 10
Supporting Healthy Brain Chemistry

If a man loudly blesses his neighbor early in the morning, it will be taken as a curse.

— Proverbs 27:14 (NIV)

Some of the proverbs recorded in Scripture are a bit perplexing. Of course they are all inspired and full of wisdom and practical insight, but some seem a bit unusual particularly when viewed through our modern lens. Still, as we look closer we can discover many insightful principles and lessons for our kids and us.

The lesson offered in Proverbs 27:14 is one of those intriguing and perplexing insights. Certainly, it has a number of possible interpretations, but as we have learned more about the brain chemistry of at-risk children, I have become aware of one possible interpretation or explanation that also applies to them.

The Body Matters

Neurotransmitters are the chemical messengers that help our bodies think, feel and move. They are involved in virtually all of our bodily functions. At the right levels, we experience optimal energy, mood, thinking and learning. However, as detailed in Chapter 10 of *The Connected Child,* when neurotransmitter levels are too high or too low, physical, emotional, behavioral and cognitive challenges can arise.

In this proverb involving the loud, overly friendly man we see a situation that can be interpreted as similar to what many of our children experience. The neighbor's day started off 'out of balance,' and that lack of balance was taken as an assault and a curse. Likewise, many of our children's bodies—in particular, their brain chemistry—are out of balance. As a result, it often seems that their days end up cursed, so to speak. In turn, our children can become overly prone to irritability, volatility, whining and so much more, all of which gives rise to behaviors and coping strategies that push us away rather than invite us to move in close and connect.

As we discussed earlier in this study guide, Scripture clearly speaks to the importance of our whole being—body, soul and spirit. Jesus often focused his teaching on the physical body and its needs.

We see this in Scripture, for example, in the Lord's model prayer, teaching about fasting, references to water and "Living Water," Jesus feeding hungry crowds (both spiritually and physically) and the need for nourishment of the soul through various spiritual disciplines. In addition, we see that one aspect of the body's needs (i.e., the need for food) was one of the ways Jesus himself was tempted by Satan in the wilderness (Matthew 4:1-3). We are created as "whole beings," and just as Jesus did not ignore the importance of the body, neither should we.

All too often, however, we do ignore the profound importance of the condition of our children's bodies to their detriment. Because of their histories, our children are much more likely to have imbalances in their brain chemistry, which makes them more susceptible to all forms of stressors. Being aware to support their "whole being," and especially their brain chemistry, can become an effective part of providing the practical and holistic nurture our children need. What's more, research has found that we can actually improve brain chemistry in children from hard places through interventions designed to reduce fear, engage them in sensory rich activities, provide healthy touch and enhance connections.

Empowered to Succeed

By Dr. Karyn Purvis

I recently spoke with a mother about her son, Tommy. Tommy is a child from a hard place and was adopted at age two. This mother had become exceedingly frustrated because it seemed as though Tommy was determined to sabotage every family activity and outing. Even on his birthday, with friends and presents all around, Tommy managed to melt down when one little thing didn't go exactly his way. "Why couldn't Tommy just enjoy the good times?" this sweet mom wanted to know.

I explained to her that many of our children are simply unable to distinguish between "good" and "bad" stress. In other words, their bodies cannot differentiate whether the stress they are experiencing is a result of a joyful, happy moment or flooding over them because of fear and anxiety. This is why so many of our kids experience "meltdowns" after happy moments such as birthday parties, accomplishing something new (e.g., learning to ride a bike) or even holidays. In fact, these effects aren't necessarily limited to the same day, but can occur days before or after an exciting event, such as the beginning of school or bringing home a straight-A report card.

Knowing this tendency, I encouraged the mother to begin to anticipate this reaction from Tommy and, more importantly, to become proactive and intentional about helping him be able to manage his stress—whether the stress was "good" or "bad." I explained to her the need to give Tommy voice so that he could express how he was feeling and to find ways to help Tommy calm himself. In addition, we discussed the importance of making sure that Tommy did not get over-tired as well as the need to help him avoid a dip in his blood sugar level by providing him a nutritious snack at several points during the day (i.e., roughly every two hours). Most important, I encouraged her to keep in mind that Tommy's behavior, while unacceptable, likely had to do with much more than just him willfully misbehaving.

Parents of children like Tommy need to be sure they are empowering their children to succeed by focusing on the whole child, including nutrition, hydration, sleep and other physical needs. The temptations for our kids to melt down are often very great, but we have the ability to empower them with the tools and strategies they need to overcome these temptations.

Key Scripture Verses

The Gospel accounts record many instances in which Jesus encountered people with both physical and spiritual needs. Mark captured one such example in Mark 6 as Jesus fed the crowd of five thousand:

The apostles gathered around Jesus and reported to him all they had done and taught. Then, because so many people were coming and going that they did not even have a chance to eat, he said to them, "Come with me by yourselves to a quiet place and get some rest."

So they went away by themselves in a boat to a solitary place. But many who saw them leaving recognized them and ran on foot from all the towns and got there ahead of them. When Jesus landed and saw a large crowd, he had compassion on them, because they were like sheep without a shepherd. So he began teaching them many things.

By this time it was late in the day, so his disciples came to him. "This is a remote place," they said, "and it's already very late. Send the people away so they can go to the surrounding countryside and villages and buy themselves something to eat."

But he answered, "You give them something to eat."

—Mark 6:30-37 (NIV)

Building Upon a Strong Foundation

As we mentioned, it is important that parents focus on the holistic needs of their children in order to empower them and create a strong foundation for their future growth and success. As Christian parents we are often keenly focused on the importance of feeding our children spiritually, and rightly so, but we must remember that another key aspect of this strong foundation is meeting their unique physical needs. We must recognize that even when a child's spirit may be willing, the body may simply be too weak. This is a reality of the human condition, and we must recognize that it is more likely to affect and inhibit children from hard places.

We see the reality that the body matters exemplified in Jesus' earthly ministry. Time and time again, as evidenced by the passage from Mark 6, we see Jesus focused on meeting the physical needs of people even as he focused on their spiritual needs. Our focus should be no less holistic when it comes to our children. By remaining focused on our whole child—body, soul and spirit—we can best help them grow and heal.

Questions to Consider and Discuss:

1. How much consideration have you given to your child's brain chemistry and physical needs in terms of understanding his/her behavioral issues and what may be contributing to them?

2. Have you seen behaviors or other indications that have caused you to wonder if your child's brain chemistry is out of balance or if other physical needs are not being adequately met?

3. Based on the fact that research has determined that brain chemistry can be altered with interventions (such as the ones taught in *The Connected Child*), what connecting strategies and interventions should you consider utilizing with your child?

Chapter 11
Handling Setbacks

The LORD is compassionate and gracious, slow to anger, abounding in love.

— Psalm 103:8 (NIV)

God's history with mankind is a history of Him dealing with our faults, failures and sin. Were it not for His great patience with us and the setbacks we experience, the story of man would have been one very brief chapter. Even as we look at the "heroes" of the Bible, we find this list of great men and women replete with those who failed and yet found strength in God's grace to try again. Moses, Elijah, Sampson, David and Peter—we see God time and time again graciously and mercifully extending opportunities for "re-do's."

Being Intentional to Remember

As loving parents, we know our children learn just like we do—through trial and error. When babies first start to walk, we understand they will fall many times before they are steady on their feet. We understand that even into adulthood there will be occasions when we will stumble and fall.

For parents of at-risk children, setbacks can be particularly discouraging, but they are an unavoidable and even necessary part of the journey. It is always important in the face of these setbacks to remember just how far you and your child have come.

After starting a therapeutic home-based program, the mother of an aggressive 11-year-old boy kept a log on her calendar to track changes in his behavior. She recorded an "A" for the good days and a "B" for the not-so-good ones. Below are the results the mother recorded over a 14-week period:

Week 1:	BABBBBB
Week 2:	BBBBBAB
Week 3:	BAABABB
Week 4:	BBBBBBB
Week 5:	BBBBBBB
Week 6:	AABBBAA

Week 7:	ABAAAAB
Week 8:	AAABABA
Week 9:	AABABAA
Week 10:	BAAAAAA
Week 11:	BAAABAA
Week 12:	ABBAABA
Week 13:	AAABABA
Week 14:	AAAABAA

As you can see, this troubled child started with only one good day for each of the first two weeks and after a little progress the following week he experienced a significant setback (in weeks 4 and 5). But his parents refused to give up, and as a result they began to see dramatic progress after only a few more weeks. By the end of 14 weeks, the original trend had completely turned around, with the child having only one not-so-good day during the final week. As time went on, if either of them became discouraged by setbacks this mother would pull out the calendar to remember just how far they had come by working together and consistently applying the approach we advocate in *The Connected Child*. This tangible reminder gave them the hope as well as the motivation they needed to keep going.

We see an example of this type of intentional remembering in the Old Testament practice of observing the Shabbat, or the holy day of rest also known as the Sabbath. Shabbat was a special celebration focused on faith and family. The family table was traditionally adorned with special settings and candles, and special foods were prepared. Shabbat was also a time for family celebration in which the father would play games with the children. This special day served as the anchor for the entire week. Three days before Shabbat the parents would speak with their children about its coming, reminding them of all they would do on that day. Preparations began with the children helping cook foods and prepare the arrangements. Most importantly, Shabbat was a day of remembering all that God had done. Observance of Shabbat in this very intentional manner allowed this holy day to permeate the week and reflected what some have called the "rhythm of the sacred"—to *hope/anticipate* for three days of preparation, to *experience/celebrate* Shabbat and then to *remember/reflect* for the three days following.

Because of their early histories, many of our children have few happy memories of their past, and all too often they have little hope for their future. Setbacks are likely to create a sense of hopelessness in them. That is why it is so important that parents practice this principle of remembering with their children. We must remember how far we have come and all that God has done to make that possible. This kind of intentional remembering can become an effective tool for guiding both you and your child through the inevitable setbacks that are part of the adoption journey.

Getting on the Right Track

By Michael & Amy Monroe

We know that children from hard places react in one of three ways when their fear response is activated: fight, flight or freeze. Our son, Carter, now five years old, was adopted from Guatemala, and from the time that he came home his response to fear, stress and pain has always been flight. As we sometimes say, he's a runner.

When he was younger, if he got into a tiff with his siblings and got his feelings hurt or if he simply didn't get his way, he took off. If we asked him to do something he didn't want to do or got onto him for misbehaving, he would react by trying to escape and hide. Over time this response became so pervasive that even when he would fall and get hurt he would run through the house and hide, while crying hysterically.

Unfortunately, we didn't always recognize this response for what it was—a fear response. We would often scold or discipline him for running off or try to ignore him altogether, but neither approach worked to calm him or resolve the situation. As Carter grew a bit older, these episodes became more frequent, to the point that they occurred nearly every day. Sometimes they would escalate and last nearly an hour, and occasionally even longer. One instance began when Carter was playing ball outside and fell and skinned his knee. Immediately he began crying hysterically, his body becoming rigid as he screamed and yelled. As we approached him to check his injury, he was unable to run off and escape so instead he became verbally and physically aggressive.

We were frustrated but wanted to help him, so shortly before Carter turned four we began responding to these episodes very differently. In response to incidents that would usually send Carter fleeing, we would quickly go to him and try to calm him using an abundance of nurture. As we held him close, patted him and even rocked him at times, we were also quick to lovingly encourage Carter to try to calm himself and use his words to tell us what had happened or where he was hurt. Almost immediately, we began to see significant improvement. While Carter's instinctive response is still to flee in reaction to being hurt, mistreated or slighted, he is now better able to calm himself and explain what happened, often returning to play in only a few minutes.

Running away had been his standard response for nearly three years with no signs of improvement. But when we decided to handle these situations differently, his reaction improved dramatically, and he began to master new ways to cope. Make no mistake, Carter is still a runner—but now he doesn't always run and when he does he typically doesn't "go far." Even though he is still inclined to return to his old habits and behaviors (sometimes at the most inopportune or embarrassing moments), the progress has been remarkable and we are quick to remember and remind him of that. More important, we are now better prepared to handle those times when he (and we) revert back to the old way of responding because we are mindful of our progress, and we are confident that together we are on the right track.

Key Scripture Verses

Consider it a sheer gift, friends, when tests and challenges come at you from all sides. You know that under pressure, your faith-life is forced into the open and shows its true colors. So don't try to get out of anything prematurely. Let it do its work so you become mature and well-developed, not deficient in any way. If you don't know what you're doing, pray to the Father. He loves to help. You'll get his help, and won't be condescended to when you ask for it.

—James 1:2-5 (*The Message*)

Needing Help and Asking for It

I love the opening words in the Book of James. They are refreshingly honest and encouraging, especially for parents with children from hard places. These words remind us that God is at work in the very midst of the trials of life, both taking away from (refining us under pressure) and adding to (maturing and developing our character) who we are so that we may ultimately become more like Him.

James also makes clear that God is ever ready to hear our cries for help and is willing and able to respond. In fact, James tells us, "He loves to help" (James 1:5, *The Message*). So why has it become unacceptable—even a sign of weakness or failure—for parents of children from hard places to need or seek help? Tragically, this tendency seems to be prevalent in more than a few of our churches, where the pressure to be "normal" and have kids who are always well-behaved can be almost overwhelming. This pressure is often acutely felt by adoptive and foster parents.

Based on what we know of Scripture, this aversion to admitting the need for help and being willing to seek it is neither biblical nor healthy. The fact of the matter is that all families who adopt and foster children from hard places will need help from their family, friends, church family and certainly their Heavenly Father. This help, in ways both large and small, must always be practical and should be offered freely without judgment or shame. After all, if God loves to help in the midst of our trials, shouldn't His children be willing and even eager to do the same?

As followers of Christ, we know that in this world we will have trouble (John 16:33). In the Gospels we are reminded that following Christ is costly, and following Him along the adoption journey will certainly be no different. Yet, we know that following Christ, no matter what the cost, is always worth it. We know God is at work in all things to accomplish His purposes, and the trials, suffering and setbacks of the adoption journey are no exception. There is hope and there is help; parents need to seek and cling to both.

Questions to Consider and Discuss:

1. What setbacks are you currently dealing with in your adoption or foster care journey? What setbacks are you currently dealing with in your life in general?

2. How do you see God at work in the midst of these setbacks?

3. What challenges are you facing for which you need help from others? Where can you turn for that help? What is preventing or holding you back from seeking or accepting that help?

4. List three ways in which your child's behavior and/or your relationship with your child has improved, no matter how small or seemingly insignificant.

5. What are some ways that you can be more intentional about "remembering" your child's progress and successes?

Chapter 12
Healing Yourself to Heal Your Child

Praise be to the God and Father of our Lord Jesus Christ, the Father of compassion and the God of all comfort, who comforts us in all our troubles, so that we can comfort those in any trouble with the comfort we ourselves have received from God.

— 2 Corinthians 1:4 (NIV)

As a young child, my family traveled deep into Mexico to accompany my father on a business trip. While he attended meetings, our mother and the children were able to go sightseeing. One particular memory from this trip has lingered in my mind for many years.

While visiting a beautiful church on one of our sightseeing excursions, we noticed platforms on each side of the centuries-old structure. Asking our guide about the platforms, he explained that there were many converts to Christianity among the native people who lived in the nearby mountains. The platforms had been erected on the sides of the church so when they came down from the mountains to worship God, they could also perform rituals to the sun god, fertility goddess and other pagan deities.

As a child I was struck by how odd this custom seemed. There was nothing in my cultural or religious background that made such a practice even remotely familiar. I remember wondering how it was that these people could have come to believe in and worship God, while at the same time still be so tied to their past beliefs and traditions. Yet in the Old Testament the children of Israel, called by the one true God, repeatedly fell into worshipping and yielding their allegiance to other gods (e.g., Numbers 25 and Judges 2). By our nature we are people prone to have divided loyalties, so to speak. In a similar manner, many of us experience adoption into the family of our Heavenly Father through faith in Jesus Christ, but we continue to be heavily influenced, and in some cases bound, by patterns from earlier in our lives and by the brokenness of this world.

Facing the Past, Finding Hope for the Future

We find that parents often minimize the importance of what they themselves bring to the table when it comes to parenting and connecting with their children. After all, the past is in the past and there is nothing we can do to change it, right? As Lewis Smedes writes in *The Art of Forgiving*, "One of God's better jokes on us was to give us the power to remember the past and leave us no power to undo it."

Experience has shown and research reinforces that although this important topic may be often overlooked, it is foundational for parents in establishing strong and enduring connections with their children to help them overcome their past wounds and present challenges. Many of our children come to us having experienced trauma, neglect and loss, and as a result have developed attachment styles that are anything but secure. Naturally, we want to lead our children to security and healing, but too often we discover that we do not know the way there for ourselves. The undeniable reality is that, just as with our children from hard places, our past affects our future, but the good news for us and our children is that the past does not determine our future. We must never forget that we are loved by God who is capable and intent on putting the broken pieces of our lives back together and bringing healing to our deepest wounds. It is critical, however, that parents be as intentional about dealing with their own past as they are about focusing on their child's past.

Research on parenting and attachment styles shows that there is a significant likelihood that parents will pass their attachment style and some of their own "emotional baggage" from one generation to the next, just as they themselves "inherited" the same from their parents. In fact, one of the greatest predictors of a child's attachment style is their parent's attachment style, coupled with the degree to which a parent has or has not adequately dealt with and resolved his or her past (including past losses and trauma).

Inherited Disconnect

By Dr. Karyn Purvis

Bob's childhood was a miserable one. His father was an alcoholic and an abuser. Escaping his chaotic home as a young adult, Bob married and began a family, vowing he would never treat his children like his father treated him. As a father of three, Bob was devoted to the Lord, was a man of character and adored his growing family. A leader in the church, he spent Sundays teaching Bible study, working in the church nursery and worshiping with his family. Knowing about his childhood and his devotion to his family, I was dismayed one Sunday standing in the side entrance to the church nursery where an unnerving scene unfolded.

Three-year-old Tommy stood beside his father's leg, shaking his small hand in the air, and crying steadily. His father, Bob, was enraptured in a deep theological discussion with another father who was also volunteering in the nursery. Tommy persistently continued tugging on Bob's pants, and whimpering for what seemed an interminable period of time. Finally Bob and his friend paused their discussion, and he knelt down to his whimpering son. "Tommy, what's wrong" he asked to which the preschooler replied, "My finger got hurt in the door!" With softening voice, Bob continued "Tommy, let's ask Jesus to make it feel better." After uttering a simple "healing" prayer Bob stood up and continued his theological discussion with his friend, leaving a sniffling and bewildered three-year-old standing silently by his leg.

Bob, like many other Christian fathers, is a good man and a committed father, but his childhood experiences, and his purposeful intention to be a godly father, had obscured some of the simple truths of faith. In that moment, his young son needed his immediate attention as well as practical expressions of love and care. Tommy didn't need merely a prayer with words about comfort; he needed to receive comfort. He needed to be swooped into his father's strong arms and cradled tenderly against his chest until the pain had passed. He needed to know that his father's attention would be given to him immediately when he was hurt and crying. He simply needed to be held and comforted. His dad could have had the theological discussion anytime, but opportunities to build trust and relationship with his son wouldn't always be available. Developmentally, a three-year-old can't understand abstractions; they live in a concrete world. Young children need embodied expressions of God's compassion and tenderness if they are to learn to trust His love.

What's more, it is doubtful that Bob would have reacted in the same way had he accidentally smashed his own finger in a door. More likely, he would respond naturally to the pain, by holding his injured hand with the other hand, pressing it against himself and swaying back and forth. If he had uttered a "prayer" during those moments, the words might not have been so pretty. But he would have given immediate, undivided, physical and emotional attention to the injury.

Although Bob was a committed believer he was unaware of his child's deepest needs. He would never harm his child, but he was unable to hear Tommy's voice or understand the needs he expressed. Although Bob had come to the Lord as a young father, the vestiges of his own childhood experiences prevented him from having insights about how to better nurture and connect with his son.

Leading Our Children to a Place We've Already Been

For most of us there are issues from our childhood that need to be explored, resolved and released—not only for our own sake, but also for the sake of our children. For some of us these issues involve unpleasant memories, fears or situations that caused tension in our families growing up. All in all they may seem rather insignificant. For others, however, the issues involve loss, harm, abuse and other traumatic and deeply painful experiences, which have left us emotionally wounded and scarred. All of these past hurts and issues, whether large or small, can essentially "stand between" us and our children if left unattended and unresolved. Our unresolved past has the potential to inhibit our ability to see our children's true conditions and needs and can ultimately impair our ability to connect with them. Without our knowledge or permission, our past can silently rob both us and our children.

Many people have told us their stories, but a few illustrate this issue well:

- A pastor's wife tells of how she allowed her 12-year-old son to be physically violent with her in order to show him God's unconditional love. Only later did she realize that she was repeating the pattern of her own childhood, where she grew to mistakenly accept her father's physical beatings as a sign of love.

- A missionary recounts his dismay as he realized the root of the conflict with his 8-year-old son not meeting his expectations was actually that he had adopted a child the exact age of his own brother who drowned when they were swimming together as children. Having never adequately dealt with and resolved the childhood loss of his brother, this father discovered that in a real sense he had somehow thought his son would be able to ease the aching memory and loss of his brother.

- A devout church elder shared that because his father was an alcoholic, he was determined to keep his son on the "straight-and-narrow" at all cost. Over time he realized his childhood experiences of growing up with an alcoholic parent were clouding his ability to understand his child and see who he really was.

- A precious Christian mother told me through bitter tears that as a teenager she aborted her first child and had never been able to forgive herself. Over time, she had come to realize that part of her motivation for adopting a child had been an attempt to save another child from abortion and to help heal her own pain. She now realized that in order to be fully present for her daughter she needed to accept God's forgiveness.

Each of these Christian parents is devoted to their family and seeking to follow God. Yet for each, interactions with their children were negatively affected by the burdens and pain of their early histories. These parents are not alone. We all have feet of clay when it comes to breaking free from our past. We all need to explore areas of loss and painful experiences from our childhood that may be keeping us from a joyful, healthy relationship with our children. The simple truth is that it is nearly impossible for a parent to lead a child to a place of healing if the parent does not know the way herself. Therefore, we must recognize that a critical aspect of our role in helping our children connect and heal is to travel the journey of healing ourselves.

Key Scripture Verses

All praise to the God and Father of our Master, Jesus the Messiah! Father of all mercy! God of all healing counsel! He comes alongside us when we go through hard times, and before you know it, he brings us alongside someone else who is going through hard times so that we can be there for that person just as God was there for us. We have plenty of hard times that come from following the Messiah, but no more so than the good times of his healing comfort—we get a full measure of that, too.

—2 Corinthians 1:3-5 (*The Message*)

How Do We Get from Here to There?

The path toward healing for both us and our children is one that is sure to have many ups and downs and twists and turns. It will not unfold easily or quickly, and it is a journey that we are not meant to travel alone.

Scripture makes clear that we were created to connect. With the Holy Spirit as our ever present guide, we must be willing to invite and welcome others to walk with us on this journey. Along the way we need to take time to pause, reflect and pray as we remain open and receptive to the "healing comfort" of God (2 Corinthians 1:5). But we should always remember that authentic healing—for both us and our children—will almost certainly take time. The transformation that we long for will not happen over night. It is a process, and one we must intentionally and persistently pursue with fierce honesty and a willingness to forgive.

We need to also cling to the truth that no life is too broken, no past too imperfect, no heart too wounded for our loving God to redeem and begin to heal. Jesus has extended the invitation: "Come to me, all you who are weary and burdened, and I will give you rest" (Matthew 11:28, NIV). We need to accept his invitation and find rest and hope in him and all that he has made available to us.

Fundamentally, as those who have placed our faith in Christ and been adopted into the family of God we must come to realize, maybe for the first time, that we cannot truly understand ourselves until we begin to grasp just how much we are loved by our Heavenly Father. Our truest identity, and that of our children, is found in Him. We are loved by a God of hope who himself is no stranger to the brokenness and suffering of this world. This same God desires to put the broken pieces of our lives together with the broken pieces of the lives of our children to fashion something truly beautiful and bring glory to His name.

We have been given the privilege of joining Him in this journey, and what a privilege it is. May we remain ever faithful as we travel for the sake of our children and in response to the abundant love of the One who has called us.

Questions to Consider and Discuss:

1. How much emphasis do you place on the importance of your role (including your own history and attachment style) in the process of developing a strong and secure connection with your child?

2. What issues or hurts from your past might you need to reflect on and deal with in order to be more fully present and emotionally available for your child?

3. Thinking in terms of leading your child to a place you have already been yourself, what issues or challenges is your child facing that you need to be available to help him/her begin to deal with and heal from?

4. What are some specific steps you need to consider taking in order to experience healing for yourself? What are some specific sources of help and encouragement that could benefit you?